⌂Successful Custom Interiors

⌂Successful Custom Interiors

Jane Cornell

Structures Publishing Company
Farmington, Michigan 48024

ACKNOWLEDGEMENT

We are greatly indebted to the many fine manufacturers and their public relations personnel who contributed the projects and plans for this book. They are listed in the back, so that you may contact them directly for further information. Without them, this book would never have come into being.

And special thanks are due to Chris Root for her advice and help in organizing the book; and to Evan Frances, Editor-In-Chief of 1001 Decorating Ideas, plus that fine magazine, for the use of many of the creative projects we have taken from that publication.

Manufactured in the United States of America

Book edited by Shirley M. Horowitz

Book production by Carey Jean Ferchland

Cover photo courtesy of 1001 Decorating Ideas Magazine.

Current printing (last digit)
10 9 8 7 6 5 4 3 2 1

Structures Publishing Co.
Box 1002, Farmington, Mich. 48024

LIBRARY OF CONGRESS CATALOGING IN PUBLICATION DATA

Cornell, Jane
  Successful custom interiors.

  Includes index.
  1. Interior decoration. I. Title.
NK2110.C57   643'.6   79-15910
ISBN 0-912336-87-0
ISBN 0-912336-88-9 pbk.

Contents

Stock wood moldings above the fireplace and for a chair rail complete the traditional feeling of this cozy room. Doors, windows and moldings are all painted the same color for continuity.
(Photo courtesy of Western Wood Moulding and Millwork Producers)

Introduction

Creating your own custom effects and accessories is one of the most exciting and satisfying aspects of home decorating. Custom touches can totally transform the look of your home. Customizing brings a period interior up to date, or helps to give authenticity to a room decorated in a traditional style. The addition of something custom-made—a divider, furniture piece, or accessory—may be the only element needed to pull existing furnishings into a cohesive whole.

With custom effects, no room in your home can be duplicated exactly by anyone else. Customizing is one way of saying, "This living space is uniquely and personally my own."

During the Renaissance, the well-to-do usually commissioned artisans to create unique decorative effects. It was typical and acceptable to spend years finishing a masterpiece like a frescoed wall. Even today, we all know someone who is equally committed to a spectacular home customizing project that is the source of great satisfaction to the proud "do-it-yourself" craftsperson.

One trend today is towards minimalism, with functional objects in a living space. This is in complete contrast to heavy adornment; but, with this new simplicity, the choice of each element in a room is crucial. The custom effects chosen for the simplest interiors are vitally important. Careful attention must be paid to details like the texture of walls, the use of carpeted platforms, and the size of the furniture chosen for the room.

In addition to being a media for your own personal expression, custom effects are the troubleshooters in any decorating scheme. For instance, if you are trapped in a muted color scheme with a subtle carpet color and relatively somber sofa upholstery—if your home has no zing—bring bright accessories to the rescue. A simple and relatively inexpensive solution might be to use bright throw pillows on the sofa; or introduce a colorful painting into the room; or go for broader strokes and put in an accent wall in a pretty paint, a wild wallpaper, or an elegant paneling.

One enormous advantage of adding your own custom effects is that you can get exactly what you want. Half-measures need not be accepted since you choose the colors, sizes and shapes to fit your plans exactly. Because you are doing it yourself, you can make your choices both practical and pretty. For instance, you can build a paneled wall that also doubles as a storage area. Or, you can make a lamp that is scaled to fit over the table that you want to accessorize.

The projects included in this book range from the very simple to those that require some knowledge of basic carpentry. None require a special knowledge of crafts, although "pride of creation" is a benefit of them all. In most cases, you will need very little time and talent and only a few tools to produce something truly unique. With many projects, once you have mastered the basic technique, you can use the knowledge to branch out on your own.

PLANNING ROOM BY ROOM

Successful Custom Interiors includes ideas and instructions for projects for every room. The main emphasis is on the living room. The family room is next and then the entranceways, dining areas, kitchens, bedrooms, and bathrooms. There are over a hundred projects in this book for you to use throughout your house.

If you are planning to customize your bedroom, the logical way to proceed is to turn immediately to the chapter on bedrooms. Keep in mind, however, that you may find the answer to customizing your bedroom in another chapter. You may want to use the idea exactly as explained and illustrated, or vary it slightly to suit your needs. For instance, the tables that are suggested projects in the chapter on living rooms might be just what's needed in your master bedroom or den.

Simply covered pillows in a variety of matching colors make this windowseat one that would be delightful to use. This type of carpeting comes in both roll goods and carpet squares, so you can combine both for odd spaces and save the cost of buying extra carpet yardage.
(Photo courtesy of Armstrong)

You can be equally adventurous in deciding how you want to personalize your project. A change of fabric or color, or substitution of one molding for another, can result in a vastly different look. A good example of this is what can be done with the basic cube table. You can cover it with shiny tiles for a modern look or lacquer it in Ming red to coordinate with an Oriental motif. You can paint it a flat white, causing it to practically disappear into a matching wall and keeping contrast to a minimum, or stencil it with a Pennsylvania Dutch design for a country look. You may want to cover it with a floral pastel fabric to match your bedspread, for a feminine ambience, or turn the cube into a game table by painting a chess and checkers grid on the top. Covering it with paneling to match the wall will give it a built-in appearance, and wrapping it with carpeting will result in a soft and highly textured feel and make the cube suitable for seating.

The same cube design can be enlarged to "almost room size" or reduced to serve as a plant stand. Plus, there is no rule that says a basic box must be a cube. Elongated horizontally, it becomes a loveseat/bench, and elongated vertically it becomes a statue base.

Wherever possible, suggestions are included for alternative ways of utilizing the project plans to take full advantage of their versatility.

The creative effect of any project you undertake becomes yours the moment you make the decision to try doing it yourself.

Note: We have tried to check and double check the sizes and directions included in this book to provide you with accurate information. It is always wise to read through instructions carefully and check them for yourself before undertaking any project. Structures Publishing and the author will not be responsible for any illness, injury, damages, claims, suits, actions or loss of any kind whatsoever or however caused, arising from the use or misuse of the information and/or drawings contained herein.

1
Entrances and Exits

A first impression sets the mood for your home, so make the main entrance warm and inviting. The same applies to other often-used entrances, such as the doors for the patio or backyard.

A personalized entrance is more than just looks alone; practical matters must be accounted for and family needs considered. Convenient storage for family outer wear, plus someplace to put guest clothing, can supplement an overcrowded hall closet. A piece of furniture or a built-in storage space can take the overload. A place to perch when taking off muddy boots or putting on snowshoes might turn an inconvenient foyer into a welcome one. And you will probably want a mirror of some sort unless you have a powder room nearby.

Plants have been a symbol of welcome since early Roman times, and are popular additions to many entrance foyers today. They need lighting for proper growth, however; the addition of this illumination can also act as a dramatic accent to a small foyer.

Practicality demands that flooring in an entrance be easily cleaned, and that it show tracking and dirt less than any other area in your home. Choose your foyer flooring with an eye to convenience. You will find many materials that are both practical and attractive.

This chapter contains projects and ideas that will turn the dullest entryway into a small area of grace. Included are:

- methods of dressing up doors with paint and molding;
- a hall rack and umbrella stand combination you can make;
- easy drawers that install underneath stairs;
- floor planters to hold plants;
- a lighting track that dramatizes greenery;
- resilient flooring that installs easily.

EASY DRESS-UPS

If your door just keeps the weather out, it is time to take action. Like an artist's blank canvas, doors are waiting for the creative touch. Since painting is the least expensive method of personalizing a door, your budget may suggest that you take this tack first. Otherwise, consider the hundreds of variations you can create through the use of molding, either alone or in combination with conventional coverings or paint.

Decide first whether you want your door to blend into the room's or hallway's existing scheme, or whether it should be a star within its own environment. Take cues from the rest of the room to inspire your own design. Consider repeating a shape from a dominant piece of furniture, or the pattern of your carpet or wallpaper. Certainly be mindful of the color combination of the room into which the door enters.

While these suggestions are for entrance doors, you can adapt them for use throughout your house, for inside doors and in some cases for creating a distinctive outer door. Keep in mind when finishing a door that the edges should continue the color of the room into which the door opens. For instance, if you are decorating the inside of your foyer door with dark brown paint, but the exterior door is white, the door edges should also be dark brown so that the door keeps its decorative integrity when opened into your brown foyer.

MAKE TROMPE L'OEIL PANELS

On Walls and Entrance Door

Deception can be fun when everyone is in on the visual joke. A case in point is this treatment of walls and a door; it looks like exotic paneling under

1. Draw the outline of the pretend panel insets on the walls and door–in this case, a rectangle with the top corners angled at 45 degrees. You can vary the width of the panels to fit the wall space available, but keep the same dimensions on all angled corners, (a 10" strip of molding lies between the two angles at the top corners.)

2. Paint surfaces exclusive of the part to be "paneled" in the background color. Paint door edge. Allow to dry. (Mask just-painted edges once paint is completely dry in order to protect from next paint application.)

3. Paint inside section of the "panel" in the lighter shade and allow to dry completely.

4. You will cause all panels to appear as if an imaginary light were shining on them from the same direction, casting shadows on the molding (in this case, from the left). Use the darker colored tape on the left side and top. Use the white on the right side and bottom.

5. To create the most realistic illusion, use two widths of each tape color, such as 1½" and ¾". To frame "panels," use the wider tape for the bottom and left-hand side, and the

narrower width for the right side and top.

6. For each panel, start at the bottom with wide white tape. Square off the ends and place tape along outline, extending into "panel" color. Then apply narrower white tape to right-hand side of "panel", squaring off the end where it meets the diagonal section.

7. Apply narrow tape to top right diagonal section, overlapping it on the end of the white tape. Cut through both tapes to create an angle, and remove excess tape ends. Press tape ends down firmly, so that they seem to form a continuous line. Repeat the procedure with diagonal tape in right-hand corner and tape of same width applied over the top edge.

8. Apply wider dark tape to diagonal corner on the left side, overlapping the top strip. Cut from the outside corner to inside corner through both tapes; remove excess ends, and press firmly into position.

9. Repeat the same procedure in applying wider dark tape along the left-hand side of the "panel," ending with a diagonal cut from inside to outside corners where wide dark tape meets wide white tape at the bottom.

dramatic lighting, but actually is a masterful combination of paint and colored tapes.

A decrepit old mirrored wardrobe was rescued and refurbished for use in the foyer, and the mirror on it suggested the shape to be used for the "panels." This shape is simple, and one you can use yourself. Or you can use the same technique to personalize your walls and door with any shape that better suits your fancy. The design was created by Jim de Martin (*for 1,001 Decorating Ideas*).

Tools and materials. Two shades of paint (tobacco brown and beige were used here); decorative tape in a darker color (espresso brown was used) along with white; plus regular painting gear.

Variations

- Cover the insert "panel" with either fabric or wallcovering.
- Use stark black and white tape on darkly colored walls and doors, or when you want to create an illusion of depth on an overall pattern such as a pillow ticking stripe.
- Use subtle colors of tape that vary only slightly from the two print colors, instead of dark tape and white.
- Create a trellis design by applying crossed strips of tape inside the "panel."
- Use cutouts from a wallcovering (such as floral bouquets) as center medallions within the "panel."
- Make top and bottom "panels" instead of one big one.
- Use more than one strip of tape on each side, to simulate an even wider and deeper "molding" effect.
- Use same-size tapes in the same color around the entire molding for a more stylized and easier treatment.

Alternate: Make a Door That is Always Open

There is no danger anyone will walk out of this door that is open when closed, because it is a Dutch door stylized painting. Good for game room exits, the design is bright and cheery when barn red is used with black hardware, and a glimpse of green grass and ever-blue skies are seen beyond the top half.

Tools and materials. Flat household paint in door and frame color (barn red or your choice); black for

EACH SQUARE = 8 SQUARE INCHES

Create an open door with paint. Add your own landscape on view outside the open upper half. (Courtesy of 1,001 Decorating Ideas)

1. Over solid paint, transfer the design directly to the door, using a yardstick and pencil. Make a paper pattern for hinges and place pattern where real hinges naturally go. (Use the scale to transfer to standard door or vary slightly to fit your size.)

2. Paint green grass, then blue sky. You can leave them solid, or lighten the sky where it meets the grass, add clouds of white, and even add flowers to the grass.

3. Paint red on frame, door bottom, door top. Lighten red paint slightly to paint section that appears to be the top of the Dutch door bottom half. After reds are dry, mix black into red to make darker simulated "grooves" on door and allow to dry.

4. Add black painted hardware. When dry, paint on "nails" in gray, mixed from the white and black.

5. Protect with a coat of flat finish sealer.

A painted door frame and matching molding transforms any door. Inside the molding, add panels of the room's wallcovering for a totally custom effect. (Photo courtesy of Stauffer Chemical)

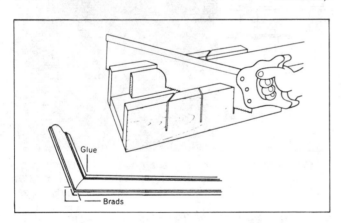

Use a miter box to miter molding sides, cutting each end on 45 degree angles in opposite directions. Glue the raw ends of both pieces together and secure the corner you create with brads. (Courtesy of Western Wood Moulding and Millwork Producers)

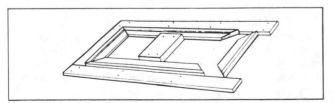

A jig frame allows you to mass produce, saving time and assuring greater accuracy. (Courtesy of Western Wood Moulding and Millwork Producers)

painted hardware; grassy green; medium blue; and white.

Variations

- Use cutouts from magazines of flowers, butterflies, or even a bird or cat to add some detail to your *trompe l'oeil* door.

ADD MOLDINGS TO YOUR DOORS

Adding real moldings to doors is a little more difficult than merely painting them, even with special treatments. However, there is no substitute for the real thing. Once you have mastered the basics of working with moldings, you will find many areas throughout your home where this expertise can be put to good use.

Disguising New Moldings

A really undistinguished foyer door can be enhanced with the addition of molding trim, especially when the panels within the molding are further decorated with wallpaper inserts. Painting the attached molding a color that contrasts with the background on the door itself disguises the fact that the molding is an addition, and not part of the original door design.

Tools and materials. White woodworking glue; 4-penny and 6-penny finishing nails; carpenter's rule; coping saw; fine sandpaper; brads; miter box and saw; putty; nail set; hammer; the molding itself.

Steps

1. Paint background color to be used on the door, and outline the design of the molding panels you plan to add. One attractive pattern has a solid horizontal panel just below the door knob, with split panels both above and below the horizontal panel, as shown. To design a pattern, sketch designs on graph paper, scaled ¼'' to the foot.

2. Determine amount of molding needed and choose an attractive molding pattern, either finished or unfinished. In estimating the amount you will need, for each mitered corner add the width of the molding to the total length. For example, if your molding is 3'' wide, and your panel has four corner miters, then add 12'' to total length; always round off to the next foot.

3. Purchase all prefinished molding at the same

time to assure a uniform match. For safe measure, buy extra molding. It is sold in many lengths, from 3' on up, so you do not have to waste much.

4. If you plan to finish many doors with identical panels, it might be worth your while to make a jig. A jig enables you to use the techniques of mass production, and is necessary in projects that require "picture framing" techniques of extreme accuracy. The jig is a mold in which frames can be made more rapidly, accurately, and uniformly.

   The inside dimensions of the jig equal the outside dimensions of the molding frame. The jig consists of stock pieces of lumber nailed to any flat, nailable surface. Sides of the jig should be tall enough to give support to the molding, but short enough to allow you to drive nails into the molding at corners to secure the pieces. Stock lumber "blocks" can be used where necessary to straighten moldings against the sides of the jig. The blocks are cut to the inside dimensions of the frame to be created. The addition of a block of wood the exact size of the inner dimension of the molding frame stabilizes the entire unit for accurate nailing.

5. With or without a jig, you will want to miter the corners for a professional look. To make square corners, set your miter box saw at 45° angles. When joined, the two pieces form a tight right angle of 90°. To make corners that are less than 90°, adjust your miter cuts to an angle wider than 45°. For angles wider than 90° (such as those needed for a hexagon), adjust and miter edges to an angle narrower than 45°.

6. For a square panel, measure and miter all four sides. Sandpaper any rough edges along miter cuts. Cover miter cuts at each corner with white wood glue and press together (an easy step with a jig). Secure the corners by nailing them together with brads from the sides of the molding. Countersink nails and cover with putty, or use nails that match the molding, and be careful to place nails flush to side surface.

7. If you are using a contrasting paint color on the molding, apply paint before attaching moldings to the door. Reserve some additional paint for any necessary touch-up work.

8. Attach molding to the door using nails, the size depending upon the size of the molding. Nail molding at corners. A colored putty stick may suffice for disguising nails at corners, or you may want to touch up your painting job.

A medium-sized pattern that allows for repeats such as this is a choice in good scale. (Photo courtesy of Stauffer Chemical)

9. To fill in the panels created by the molding with wallcovering, cut pieces slightly larger than the panel insert. Apply according to the wallcovering manufacturer's instructions, and cut the covering that overlaps onto molding with a sharp utility knife. Burnish to secure.

Variations

There is virtually no limit to the kinds of door treatments you can create with molding. The only limitation to keep in mind is that the door design you choose should be in keeping with the overall design of your furnishings and room style.

- Combine moldings with mirrors, mirror tiles, or fabric.
- Combine moldings with stock wood or other molding types.
- Be adventurous in your painting treatment with molding. For example, you can use one color for background, another for molding, and a third for the interior of the panel.

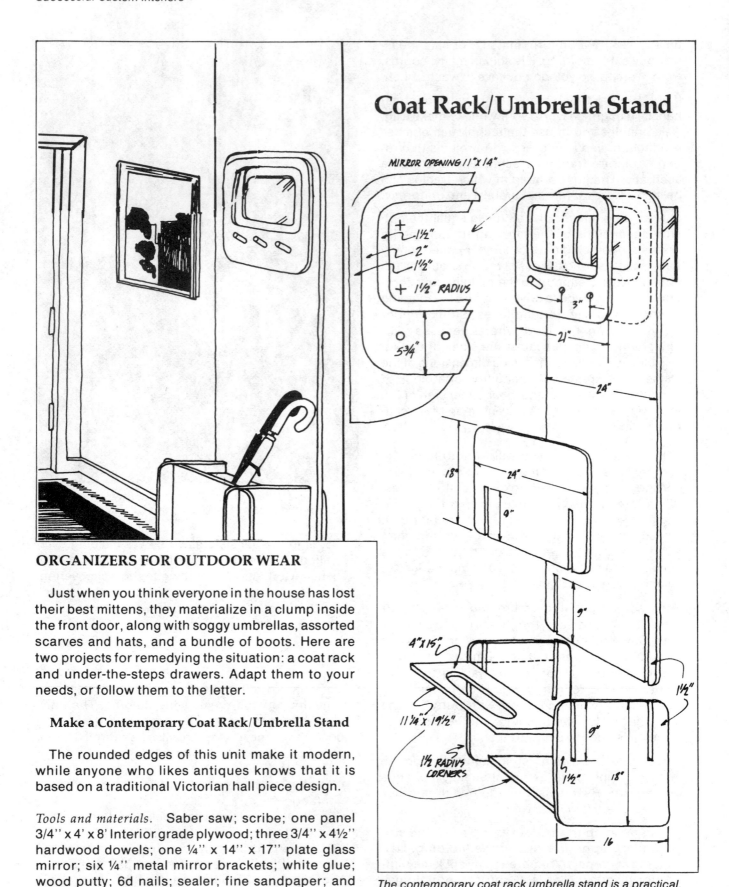

Coat Rack/Umbrella Stand

ORGANIZERS FOR OUTDOOR WEAR

Just when you think everyone in the house has lost their best mittens, they materialize in a clump inside the front door, along with soggy umbrellas, assorted scarves and hats, and a bundle of boots. Here are two projects for remedying the situation: a coat rack and under-the-steps drawers. Adapt them to your needs, or follow them to the letter.

Make a Contemporary Coat Rack/Umbrella Stand

The rounded edges of this unit make it modern, while anyone who likes antiques knows that it is based on a traditional Victorian hall piece design.

Tools and materials. Saber saw; scribe; one panel 3/4'' x 4' x 8' Interior grade plywood; three 3/4'' x 4½'' hardwood dowels; one ¼'' x 14'' x 17'' plate glass mirror; six ¼'' metal mirror brackets; white glue; wood putty; 6d nails; sealer; fine sandpaper; and semi-gloss enamel to suit.

The contemporary coat rack umbrella stand is a practical, easily constructed, foyer piece. (Courtesy of Georgia-Pacific)

Steps

1. Mark the plywood and start by making one vertical cut 24'' wide and 8' long. Divide this piece into two; one length of 76'' and the other 18'' long. These are the back and front panels.

2. Cut two pieces measuring 18'' x 16'' (sides), one piece 21¾'' x 21'' (mirror frame), and two pieces 11¼'' x 19½'' (bottom and umbrella stand).

3. Start with the mirror frame piece (21¾'' x 21''). To make the mirror opening, scribe a rectangle measuring 17'' x 14'', 2'' in from one 21'' side and 2'' in from both 21¾'' sides, off center. Draw in 3'' radius corners, drill ½'' holes at each of the corners, and cut them out with a saber saw. On the same piece, cut the outside corners using a 5'' radius as a guide.

4. On the back piece, measure down 5'' from the top of the 24'' x 76'' piece, and 5'' in from each side, and scribe 11'' x 14'' rectangle. Mark corners with 1½'' radius, drill and cut.

5. Round all corners in a 1½'' radius on the front board (24'' x 18''), and both side boards (16'' x 18''). Leave umbrella board and bottom squared.

6. Put in slots. They are all 9'' x ¾'', and are placed 1½'' in from the panel edges. Place two slots on bottom of front panel, two slots on the bottom of the back panel, and two slots on top of each side panel.

7. Cut out umbrella hole, measuring 4'' x 15'' on one horizontal 11¼'' x 19½'' piece. Round corners of cut.

8. Fill all plywood edges with wood filler and sand smooth.

9. Attach mirror frame to back panel by centering opening over opening in back panel. Nail and glue securely.

10. For coat hooks, drill three ¾'' holes at a slight angle through both frame and back panel, placed 3'' apart, centered. Cut three ¾'' dowels 4½'' long. Line the holes with white glue and insert dowels.

11. Assemble, nail, and glue slotted pieces, creating a box to hold umbrellas. Add back panel.

12. Seal the entire unit with sealer. Sand and paint.

13. Attach 14'' x 17'' plate glass mirror to the back, using metal mirror brackets.

Variations

- Place a round-cornered board over the box and add a pillow for seating.

- Paint unit with a variety of colors; edges one tone, each panel another.

- Cover some surfaces with foil paper to create an Art Deco feeling.

- Leave corners unrounded and embellish with molding.

- Cover panels with wallcovering or fabric.

ADD DRAWERS UNDER THE STAIRCASE FOR STORAGE

A new system of ready-made drawers and a rugged metal mounting frame lets you put drawers almost anywhere you have depth within the walls. The drawers come in two widths to fit between 16'' x 24'' stud spacing in home construction. A prime candidate is that unused space beneath a staircase, often overlooked in the foyer.

Tools and materials. Drawermaster drawer kit; hammer; screwdriver; level; jigsaw or foxtail saw; drill for holes; and drawer handles.

Variations

- Make a basic cube in which to attach drawers to create a free-standing unit in any dimension that will fit in your foyer.

- Decorate the drawers with paint or elegant hardware, for your personal customized effect. Or, conversely, use inconspicuous hardware and drawer fronts to disguise the drawers.

- Color code the drawers so that each family member has a drawer for mittens, scarves, and outdoor gear in general.

How to Create Built-in Drawers

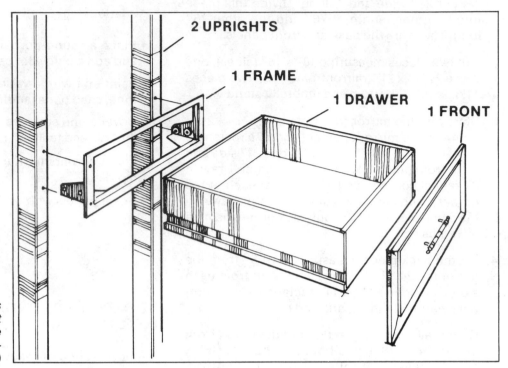

2 UPRIGHTS

1 FRAME

1 DRAWER

1 FRONT

A simple kit with drawers allows you to make use of that wasted space beneath the stairs. (Courtesy of Drawermaster)

The go-anywhere drawers that fit into the wall are available either painted or stained.

1. Find the studs in the wall and determine spacing.

2. *Use a level to establish base line for bottom drawer metal mounting frame.*

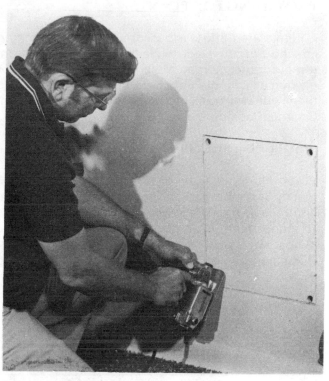

3. *Measure around perimeters of units to be installed, drill four holes in corners, and cut out and trim required holes.*

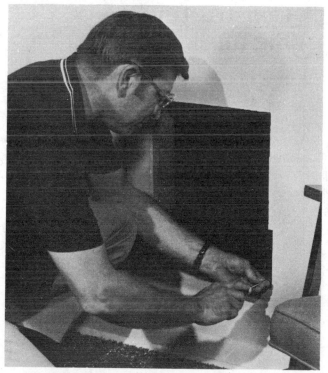

4. *Mount frames, bottom one first, by screwing them into side through wall and into stud. Positioning them flush on top of one another automatically aligns them for proper clearance.*

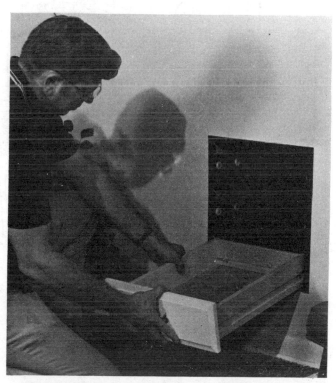

5. *Attach drawer fronts and hardware to drawers. The company makes drawer fronts in three styles, ready for painting or staining. Or you can make your own. Add drawer pulls.*

PROVIDING FOR PLANTS

Plants are perfect accessories for foyers, adding life and warmth inside while they span the gap from the outdoors. Here is a plan that includes tips for making all your planters watertight and illuminating them with wall track lighting. (The plan comes from Georgia-Pacific.)

Make a Big Block Planter

Overall dimensions of this planter design are 3 feet by 3 feet, but you can alter it to best fit your own entrance space. The supersquare shape, with sides 18 inches high, is ample enough to accommodate almost any small house tree or a variety of plants. Remember to waterproof the interior (see following project).

Tools and materials. One piece 4' x 8' x ¾'' Exterior good one side plywood; one piece 2'' x 2'' x 9' lumber; six pieces 2'' x 2'' x 10' lumber; 7d galvanized nails.

Variations

- Paint battens in contrasting color to color of planter.

- Use a contrasting stain on battens and planter.

- Decorate planter with other materials, such as decorative molding.

- Paint your own decoration on sides.

- Add coasters to bottom so that planter is movable.

Constructing the Big Block Planter

1. For planter sides, cut four pieces 18" x 35¼". With remainder of plywood, cut one piece 24" x 34½", and one piece 10½" x 34½", to make a bottom piece for the planter that will measure 34½" x 34½" square.

2. Assemble bottom pieces by nailing 2" x 2" x 34½" cleats across the split, horizontally, one in the center, and one on either end.

3. Attach 2" x 2" x 12" batten pieces to side panels as indicated in the illustration, about 1" apart. Leave off the end battens, to be attached after the box is completed, for a finished look.

4. When all sides are completed, assemble around planter as indicated in section plan. Note: each side is ¾" longer than bottom, therefore you will have an overlap of ¾" at one end. Butt this to the next panel and continue around for completion of planter box. (Courtesy of Georgia-Pacific)

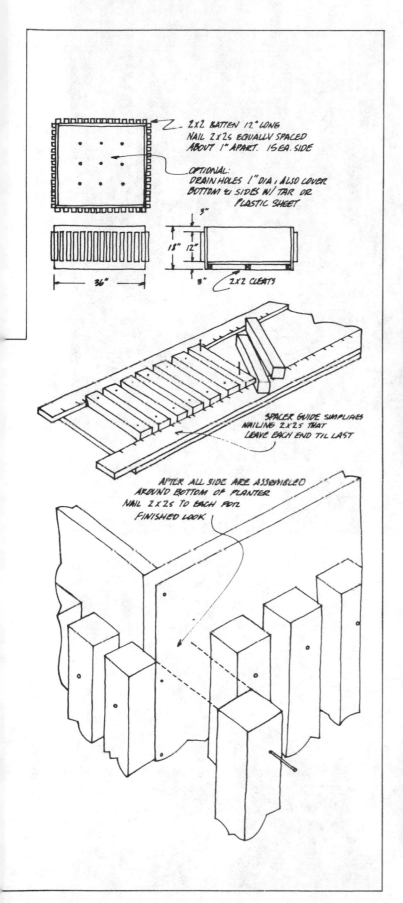

2x2 BATTEN 12" LONG
NAIL 2x2s EQUALLY SPACED
ABOUT 1" APART. 15 EA. SIDE

OPTIONAL:
DRAIN HOLES 1" DIA, ALSO COVER
BOTTOM & SIDES W/ TAR OR
PLASTIC SHEET

3"

18" 12"

36"

3"   2x2 CLEATS

SPACER GUIDE SIMPLIFIES
NAILING 2x2s THAT
LEAVE EACH END TIL LAST

AFTER ALL SIDE ARE ASSEMBLED
AROUND BOTTOM OF PLANTER
NAIL 2x2s TO EACH FOR
FINISHED LOOK

Use Roof Coating to Waterproof Your Planters

This simple treatment can save you water stains and mildew, as well as extending the life of your planters. The cured coating will not affect plants or soil.

Tools and materials. Dow Corning® silicone rubber roof coating; paint brush.

Protection Note. Seal and protect other surfaces subjected to constant water spots, such as the floor of a hall closet.

Roof coating is a simple and handy material for effectively sealing any planter. (Photo courtesy of Dow Corning)

Apply a liberal coating of silicone rubber roof coating to interior of planter. With wide gaps, seal with plastic wood on inside surface first. Allow to cure completely, and the job is done.

Track lighting is a good means of illuminating both a dark foyer corner and plants or accessories used to decorate the foyer. (Shown here is Power-Trac from Halo)

SPOTLIGHT YOUR PLANTS WITH TRACK LIGHTS

Track lights are ideal for spotlighting plants, since they can be adjusted to dramatize various arrangements and can be altered as plants grow. A vertical installation in a small hallway is one way to convert a dark corner into a plant center.

Tools and materials. Lighting track; drill; light bulbs (perhaps plant lights, if necessary because no other light is present).

1. Set track on surface. Many come in 2' module lengths.

2. *Drill two holes, making sure track is straight.*

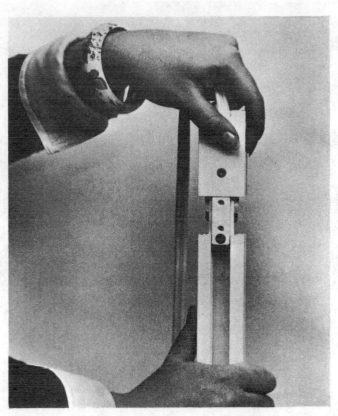

3. *Install the cord and plug connector on track.*

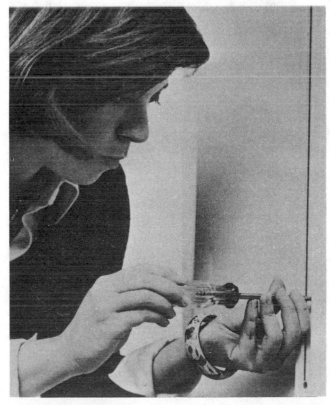

4. *Fasten unit to the wall.*

5. *Insert lampholders into track, and then adjust lampholders for best dramatization of your plants and/or other pleasing objects.*

This durable resilient flooring in sheet form has a stone pattern that makes a nice bridge from outdoors to inside. (Photo courtesy of Solarian flooring from Armstrong)

DURABLE FLOORING

Since the entrances receive the most wear and tear of any area of your home, it makes good sense to cover entrance floors with easily cleaned, easily maintained material. High on the list are the new no-wash resilient floorings. Many are designed in patterns that will disguise soil between cleanings.

Although resilient tiles are easy to install yourself, for areas that have to resist heavy water staining, solid sheet is the best choice. And for small foyers, often it is possible to find a handsome piece at a good reduction, discounted as carpet remnants are.

Install Resilient Sheet Flooring

Follow the manufacturer's instructions for types of adhesives necessary and the proper preparation of the subflooring. If you opt for the kind of sheet vinyl that merely needs to be placed down, without adhesive, the job is a snap.

Variations

- Install self-stick tiles if heavy traffic is not a problem for your foyer.
- Extend the foyer resilient flooring into an adjacent room to make both spaces seem larger.

2
Living Rooms with Character

The living room is the area where you, your family and guests congregate. When it comes to decoration, the living room is often the first room to be considered, arranged, accessorized, and generally finished. Of necessity, many of the elements that create the total effect of your living room may be purchased. However, you can achieve special effects and create custom pieces or detailing if you are modestly handy with normal workshop tools.

Living rooms often are the most formal rooms in the home; some of the projects lend themselves to a more formal environment. However, with a slight change of design, the same projects can be undertaken to create an informal appearance. With simple modifications most projects in this chapter can be used throughout the house.

Included are: wonderful wall treatments—such as creating a modern Oriental decor with molding, using screens for highly textured wallcovering, and doubling the impact with mirrors; ways to spark up your fireplace with plans for making a pressed-wood log storage cabinet and storage bench, updates for windows with pointers on mounting draperies and making lambrequins, lighted cornices, valances, and customized blinds.

Also included in this chapter are ways of making exciting fabric screens and hanging room dividers. End tables and a Parson's coffee table are diagrammed with step-by-step instructions. Smaller accessories include harem pillows for floor sitting and picture frames. Finally, basic lighting suggestions are given, plus methods of installing track lighting and ways to create your own table lamps.

WALL TREATMENTS

Walls are the largest areas in a room, so it makes good sense to pay great attention to them. Impressive wall treatments are moneysavers, because walls seldom need to be further embellished. The family will not need to acquire artworks, etc. Here are some examples of outstanding wall treatments that involve molding, unusual wall coverings, and mirrors.

Create A Modern Oriental Decor with Molding

This exciting Oriental embellishment around the windows, at the top of the walls, as a ceiling medallion, and to finish off a simple cube coffee table all comes from the humble half-round molding. The molding, usually used as a screen molding or shelf edging, is readily available at most hardware stores.

Careful measuring of the proportions and exact cutting are necessary to make this kind of geometric patterning work. Use the same motifs on flush doors, around fireplaces, for wood drapery valances, or for cabinet fronts. For maximum Oriental effect, paint the molding in traditional Oriental colors, such as Chinese red or jade green.

After mastering the techniques for making one project, you can easily adapt them to the other projects in this room. Chapter One gives not only directions for mitering molding corners, but also general molding information. The additional step necessary for these projects is coping, where one piece joins another with an uneven profile and must be shaped to join snugly. Following are directions for making a medallion at the end of a coffee table cube. Master these, and the entire technique is at your command.

Decorate a Cube

Tools and materials. White woodworking glue; 4-penny and 6-penny finishing nails; carpenter's rule; coping saw; fine sandpaper; putty; nail set; hammer, miter box, and saw; molding itself.

Molding totally transforms this room. (Courtesy of Western Wood Moulding and Millwork Producers)

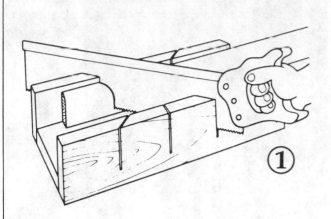

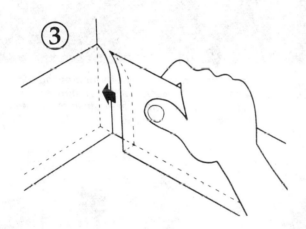

To cope a molding, make a 45 degree cut, angled so that a slanted raw edge shows from the front.

How to Cope a Molding

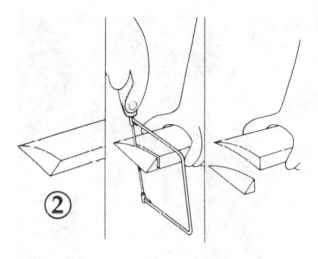

Cut straight back across the molding so that all of the slanted, raw wood is removed.

Remaining trimmed molding end will fit snugly to matching molding.

Steps

1. Paint end of cube a contrasting color, top and sides to match molding.

2. Measure and miter one rectangle to surround edges of cube.

3. Measure distance from centers of rectangle half rounds, to determine length of top crosspieces. Mark length on crosspiece top.

4. Cope four crosspieces to join the two rectangles. They should be the same length, coped so ends conform to profile of half rounds used in rectangles.

5. To do this, place half round crosspieces in miter box, back to the bottom of the box. To cope left end of crosspiece, place in miter box as illustrated, with saw blade crossing center of crosspiece where top center is marked.

6. Using a coping saw, cut straight back across the half round so that all slanted, raw wood is removed.

7. Remaining trimmed molding will fit matched molding snugly, although a little sanding may be necessary to smooth the cut.

8. Reverse angle of the coping saw in miter box and follow these same steps for the right-hand end of the crosspiece.

9. Finish all four crosspieces, adjust for joining the two rectangles, and paint the molding pieces. Attach rectangles, then coped crosspieces, with nails and glue to end of cube.

Variations

- Duplicate one of the other wall molding treatments shown.
- Make rectangles of any size to fit walls, using any manner of molding.
- Fill rectangular panels with wallpaper.
- Use molding on wall to delineate wall hangings.
- Combine stock lumber and moldings to create interesting effects.

A close-up shows simple techniques for creating panelled effect. Screen stock surfaced on four sides is applied vertically to plywood with horizontal members butting at right angles. Base cap molding trims squares for finishing touch.

Panels can be filled with wallcovering to match solid walls for an unusual treatment. Here, wallcovering patterned panels are combined with stock moldings. (Photo courtesy of Wall-Tex)

You can leave the panels you create bare and fill them with artwork—a fabulous way of creating wall interest that will not detract from beautiful furniture. (Photo courtesy of Thayer Coggin, furniture designed by Milo Baughman)

Sleek, contemporary furniture such as this slouch pit grouping calls for exciting walls. Bamboo blinds are the perfect foil. (Photo courtesy of Thayer Coggin, furniture designed by Milo Baughman)

Use Shades for Highly Textured Wallcovering

Bamboo blinds or other heavily textured shades or mats make wonderful, highly textured wallcovers. In some cases, you can merely attach them to the wall, using cup hooks at the ceiling line to hold the top poles of blinds.

Other more permanent treatments may require a more permanent means of attachment. One of these is the furring strip method.

Tools and materials. Furring strips ¼" thick; heavy-duty scissors for cutting blinds; staple gun; staples; nails or paneling adhesive for applying furring strips; nails or tacks. You may be able to glue thin shades or blinds directly to the wall or strips. Ask for appropriate adhesive in a wallcovering store.

Steps

1. Measure your room and plot layout of shade panels. If necessary, make a wall layout to be sure your estimates are accurate. Estimate amount of furring strips needed. Plan on furring surrounding windows and doorways, along baseboard and ceiling line, in each corner, and vertically at edges of each panel of shade.

2. Cut and attach furring strips to all areas mentioned above, using nails or paneling adhesive. Apply plumb and use furring to line up shades.

3. Apply first panel in corner, lining up outer edge for plumb. Trim corner edge of shade to fit snugly.

4. Lightly tack blind at top and adjust plumb. Staple securely in place across top and remove temporary tacks. Staple blind along outside furring strip, corner furring strips, and finally finish bottom edge. Staple at least every 8" along side panels, close enough for a firm hold across top and bottom. You may be able to get color-coated staples for invisible look, or staple so that staples are somewhat hidden.

5. Line up next blind plumb with the first, and continue around the room.

6. At windows and doorways, cut out opening, leaving an overhang of about 3". Attach to ceiling and side plumb lines, then carefully cut to size and staple to furring surrounding window or doorway.

7. Substitute brads if blinds are too thick for staples.

Variations

- Choose natural colors for blinds or investigate textured or stained blinds.

- Spraypaint blinds before installing them or paint after installed with a heavy roller.

- Separate each shade panel with paneling strips for stylizing.

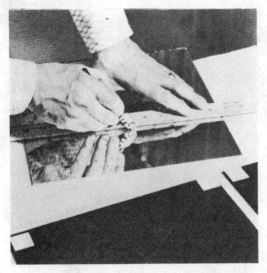

To cut mirrors, score on the right side with a glass cutter and snap. (Courtesy of 1,001 Decorating Ideas)

To place tiles on wall, first peel and apply adhesive tape to each corner of mirrors; mount on screen or wall, inserting a matchbook cover as shown for proper spacing. This allows for adjustment of mirrors to any wall movement. (Courtesy of 1,001 Decorating Ideas)

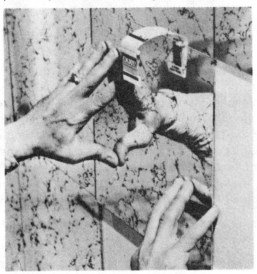

Double Your Impact with Mirrors

Mirrors can expand any room by doubling its visual size. In addition, they make the most of a view that is the natural focal point. Mirror tiles are relatively simple to install, using the manufacturer's instructions and a good bonding glue. Since mirror walls go with any decor and need only occasional cleaning, they are good investments.

Steps in determining which wall to mirror

1. Consider first what will be reflected in the mirror. Place a small mirror where the mirror wall will go, then make sure the view reflected is good from most places in the room where people sit.
2. Make sure the visual effect of a mirror wall will not make the overall room dimensions seem awkward. For example, do not put a mirror wall at the end of a long narrow room; it will make the room seem longer and narrower.
3. Make sure no one can mistake a mirror wall for the real thing, and walk into the mirror. Avoid this by placing an object in front of the mirror that is obviously repeated, such as a table or large plant.

Variations to mirror walls

- Metallic wallpaper gives a softer effect and may be the best solution when you want a feeling of expansion but no realistic reflection.
- Use strips or blocks of mirror tiles instead of an entire wallfull.
- Use mirrors or mirror tiles in the repeats of deep-set windows, and bring the outside view inside when the window is seen from an angle.

SPARK UP YOUR FIREPLACE

Fireplace tools are designed for safety first and decoration second. All accessories you make should take safety into consideration. Here are two projects, both for storage of fireplace logs, plus some suggestions for mantel and fireplace surrounds using molding.

Fireplace Bench

Separate sections hold newspapers, kindling, and logs inside this bench. With the addition of a pillow on the top, the unit becomes seating. Plans are from Georgia-Pacific.

Tools and materials. One ¾" x 4' x 8' plywood panel A-B Interior or A-C Exterior grade; two 8' x 1½" half rounds; one 4' x ¾" half round; one 4' x ¾" quarter round; 8d finishing nails; fine sandpaper; white glue; wood filler; interior semi-gloss enamel paint; cushion top.

Variations

- Construct unit from prefinished paneling to match other furniture.
- Use a contrasting color for each section of the interior.

Make a Pressed-Wood Log Storage Cabinet

Pressed-wood logs are convenient, but simply are not attractive stacked up near the fireplace. This storage cabinet keeps a good supply on hand but out of sight, and works on a hopper-feeder principle (from Georgia-Pacific).

Tools and materials. One panel ¾'' x 4' x 8' Exterior good one side grade plywood; three pieces 2'' x 4'' x 6'; one piece 2'' x 4'' x 4'; white glue; 8d nails; two metal straps; one 24''-long ¾'' x ¾'' piano hinge with screws; one wing nut with wing screw.

Steps

1. Mark all plywood pieces on panel before cutting, running face grain the long way of each piece and allowing for the width of the saw cut. Cut two side pieces with bottom curved as per plan, making a pattern for the curve of the front-feeding trough and then cutting with a saw. Cut back panel 17½'' x 36¾''. Cut front panel 17½'' x 23¾''. Cut front lip panel 7'' x 17½''. Cut top piece 19'' x 9½''.

2. Cut the left side as shown for door.

3. Cut 2 x 4s to make frame within top of feeder; four uprights 24½'' tall. Cut four front and back

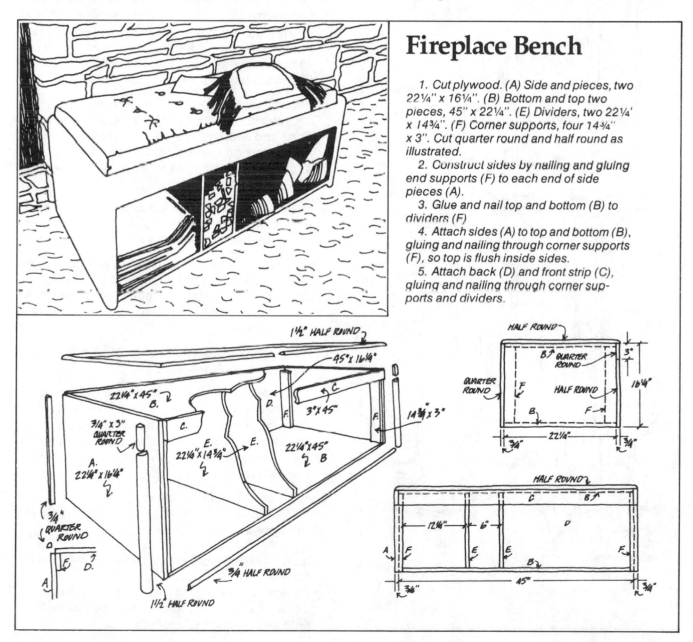

Fireplace Bench

1. Cut plywood. (A) Side and pieces, two 22¼'' x 16¼''. (B) Bottom and top two pieces, 45'' x 22¼''. (E) Dividers, two 22¼' x 14¾''. (F) Corner supports, four 14¾'' x 3''. Cut quarter round and half round as illustrated.

2. Construct sides by nailing and gluing end supports (F) to each end of side pieces (A).

3. Glue and nail top and bottom (B) to dividers (F)

4. Attach sides (A) to top and bottom (B), gluing and nailing through corner supports (F), so top is flush inside sides.

5. Attach back (D) and front strip (C), gluing and nailing through corner supports and dividers.

Log Storage Cabinet

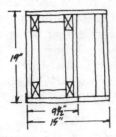

Pressed logs are practical, but not so attractive that you would want them in your living room. Use these plans to make a Log Storage Unit. From Georgia Pacific.

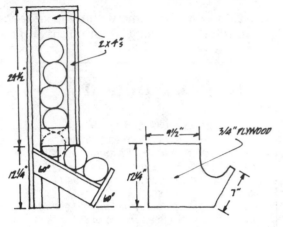

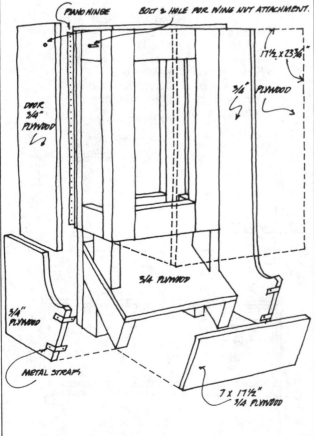

supports 11'' long. Cut four side supports 5½'' long. Nail and glue upper supports together.

4. To cut framing for bottom half of the unit, use a protractor to mark 60 degree angles. Mark directly on the lumber for diagonal supports of plywood floor. Cut slanted plywood floor 16'' wide by dimension of top of slanted 2 x 4s, and fasten to slanted 2 x 4s.

5. Place slanted floor into position, and cut two 60 degree slanted 2 x 4s to fit flush with back supports and support floor part. Cut two additional 2 x 4s to rest on slanted platform with a 60 degree angle, and position so that top is 12½'' from floor and supports top framing.

6. Fasten base framing to long 2 x 4 back supports, then fasten upper framing. Nail/glue all joints, using 8d nails and white glue.

7. Attach by gluing and nailing plywood front and back pieces, then top, then right-hand side, and bottom left side. Use metal straps to fasten angled edge of sides at bottom to 2 x 4s. Then fasten front lip panel.

8. Hang the door, using a continuous hinge along edge of back paneling.

9. To install wing nut closing, clamp door shut and drill through door and 2 x 4 frame that will hold the wing nut bolt. Insert the bolt from the inside and secure with nut, countersunk flush with the 2 x 4 so it will not turn when wing nut is used to secure door.

10. Apply sealer, paint, or stain.

Variations and suggestions

- Increase height of unit so it lines up with mantel line.
- Reverse design so that door opening is on the other side. Loading door is best placed on the side away from the fireplace.

Moldings above fireplace repeat basic mantel design.

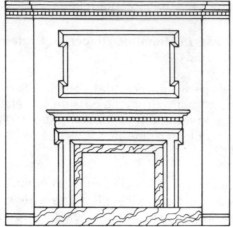

Moldings used to coordinate fireplace and wall design.

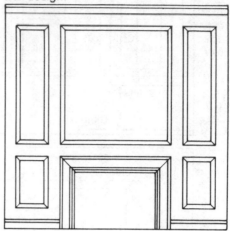

Mantel created with crown molding and S4S stock.

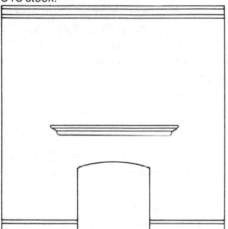

Simple mantel using S4S and crown.

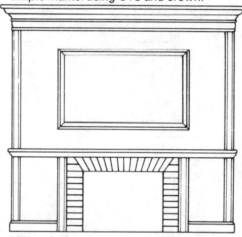

A contemporary fireplace accented by applying molding in vertical rows.

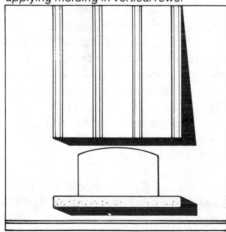

Mantel S4S and crown coordinates beautifully with applied moldings and paneling.

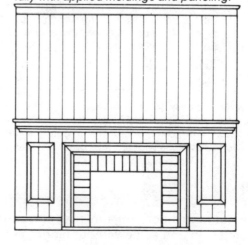

Update Your Mantel and Fireplace Surroundings

To make sure your fireplace keeps pace with the decor of the rest of your living room, consider some of these suggestions from Western Wood Moulding Manufacturer's Association. Use the same techniques for mitering wall paneling and molding to create new fireplace surroundings.

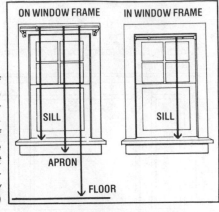

The two main methods of mounting curtains is to attach them to the window frame or inside the window frame. Your choice of methods determines the measurements you must take for a proper fit. (Courtesy of Stanley Drapery Hardware)

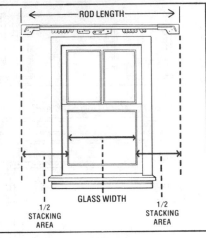

To determine the right rod length for your window with traverse rod treatments, measure the glass width. Allow your window to show fully with the draperies open, allowing for stacking area of draperies on either side of window.

Glass Width	Total Stacking Area*	Rod Length*
36"	24"	60"
48"	28"	76"
60"	32"	92"
72"	36"	108"
84"	40"	124"
96"	44"	140"
108"	48"	156"
120"	52"	172"
132"	56"	188"
144"	60"	204"

*For one-way draw, subtract 7"

The measurements in the chart are for medium weight material. For bulky fabric, add 4" to 10" to the rod length.

For other size windows, divide the glass width by 3 and add 12 inches to get the right stacking area. This figure, added to the glass width, will give you your proper rod length.

This chart shows drapery needs with medium weight material. For a one-way draw, subtract 7". For other size windows, divide the glass width by 3 and add 12" to get right stacking area. Add this to glass width to give proper rod length. (Courtesy of Stanley Drapery Hardware)

WAKE UP WINDOWS

Here are some projects for unusual structural effects—some with and some without fabrics at the windows.

Before undertaking any special window treatment, make sure you know how you will hang curtains or blinds if they are included in the plan. It often is easiest to install drapery hardware *before* complet-

ing a specialty project. While manufacturer's information included with hardware is easy to follow, here are some general guidelines.

Pointers in Mounting Draperies, Curtains, and Blinds

Outside view. Check that your window treatment will be attractive from the outside. Usually, the drapery top is mounted at least 4" above the window glass so pleater tape is not visible from your front yard.

Mix and match. A wide variety of combinations are possible, and easily installed. There are even double hardware rods specifically designed for combining draperies for special effects.

Alter apparent shape. You can hide the actual shape of a window with draperies. Extend the draperies to the sides to make a window look wider. Use floor length draperies to make windows more dominant in a room.

Window profile. A drapery that has a return of fabric turning the corner at the end and going to the wall is more attractive than curtains or draperies set away from the wall. Always consider the depth of a window treatment in figuring out your special effect.

Drawing. Decide which way is the most convenient for the draperies to draw: left side, right side, or both ways.

Measuring. Remeasure until you know you're accurate. Mounting choices for draperies include on the frame, in the frame (with cafes), on the wall, on the ceiling, or on spring-pressure mounts inside the casement. Standard lengths are to the sill (a must for curtains mounted inside the casement), to the window apron, or to the floor (with 1" subtracted for carpet clearance and slight elongation of the drapery). Allow room beside the window for stacking of draperies when they are open.

Waiting period. Wait to install hardware until after you have the draperies, to make slight adjustments necessary for proper fit.

Shades and blinds. Measure carefully. Blinds can be spacesavers, especially when installed inside the casement. They also can be installed outside the window frame, wider than the window, and to any length. They look fresh and modern on doorways.

Make a Lambrequin to Frame your Window

Lambrequins are decorative wooden constructions projecting several inches away from the wall and framing the top and sides of the window. The style of your draperies, blinds, or wallcovering are good guides for determining the best dimensions of the lambrequin. You can cut out a lambrequin with fanciful shapes on the front edge, cover it with wallcovering or fabric, finish clear, decorate, stain, or paint to match the window frame. Lambrequins make any window more impressive.

Tools and materials. Furring for frame (1 x 4s); ¼" plywood for front and sides; angle irons to attach to wall; reinforcement strips for joints; nails; good glue; staples and a staple gun for fabric-covered effects.

Steps

1. Determine overall dimensions of interior of lambrequin, making sure to leave enough room for draperies, hardware, and lighting you might install.

2. Cut two side furring strips the height of finished lambrequin. Cut two pieces to go across top and top front, width of lambrequin minus width of sides. Cut two front furring strips to height of lambrequin minus horizontal front piece.

3. Cut plywood front to fit over frame, and plywood sides.

4. Assemble frame, using nails and wood glue. Attach plywood front and sides to frame.

5. Finish lambrequin as desired. If covering with material, paint the interior first. White is a good reflective choice.

6. To cover with fabric, wrap fabric to inside surfaces and leave a 2" margin, then staple in place. If desired, wallcovering may be extended inside an equal distance.

7. Attach entire unit to wall with angle braces, after drapery hardware has been installed.

Variations

• Make an ornate lambrequin and leave the window bare.

• Add lighting inside the lambrequin similar to a lighted cornice.

Handsome lambrequins and blinds may be the only decorations your windows need. (Photo courtesy of Howard Miller)

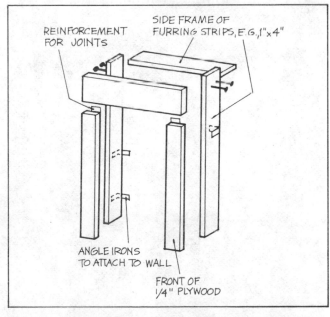

REINFORCEMENT FOR JOINTS

SIDE FRAME OF FURRING STRIPS, E.G., 1"x 4"

ANGLE IRONS TO ATTACH TO WALL

FRONT OF ¼" PLYWOOD

This expanded view shows how a lambrequin frame is made. Scale it to the proportion you need.

Make a Lighted Cornice or Valance

Cornices combine a light that is directed downward with a panel in front of the light. Commonly used with dramatic draperies to give life to windows at night, they also can be used on windowless walls. Cornices require fluorescent lights because incandescent light bulbs might overheat nearby fabrics. Cornices are effective over one window, or extended the entire length of the room. Paint the inside white for the strongest reflection. Decorate the exterior any way you wish.

Valances are similar to cornices, but with valances light is directed both downward across windows and upward to be reflected from the ceiling. The directions for installing lights within cornices and valances can be adapted for lambrequins. Follow the directions for installing lighted cornices and valances which are provided by General Electric Lamp Business Group in these illustrations.

Variations

• Use a redwood fascia for a valance or cornice to save time and effort. Dustproof tops and diffusers can be installed directly within the channel already in the fascia. Lighting fixtures can be mounted directly onto the fascia to further simplify the project.

General room illumination is provided by this valance along a contained wall. Valance uses one F30 WWX and four F40 fluorescent lamps. (Courtesy of General Electric)

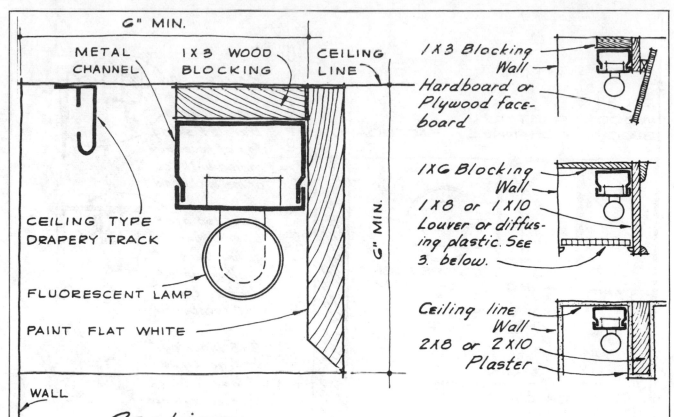

G" MIN.

METAL CHANNEL · 1X3 WOOD BLOCKING · CEILING LINE

CEILING TYPE DRAPERY TRACK

FLUORESCENT LAMP

PAINT FLAT WHITE

WALL

G" MIN.

1X3 Blocking
Wall
Hardboard or Plywood face-board

1X6 Blocking
Wall
1X8 or 1X10 Louver or diffus-ing plastic. See 3. below.

Ceiling line
Wall
2X8 or 2X10
Plaster

Section

SCALE - HALF SIZE

1. Use fluorescent lamps of the same color and tube diameter throughout (preferably from the same carton).

2. Place channel as close to faceboard as possible for best shielding. Bottom louver or diffuser is recommended when cornice is viewed lengthwise.

3. For smooth uninterrupted line of light, paint inside of faceboard flat white and use channels with white lampholders back-to-back as shown below.

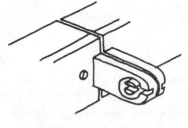

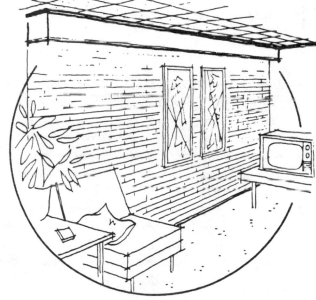

Cornices direct all their light downward to give dramatic interest to wall coverings, draperies, murals, etc. May also be used over windows where space above window does not permit valance lighting. Good for low-ceilinged rooms.

PREPARED BY · SAMUEL M. MILLS · ARCHITECT AND LIGHTING CONSULTANT

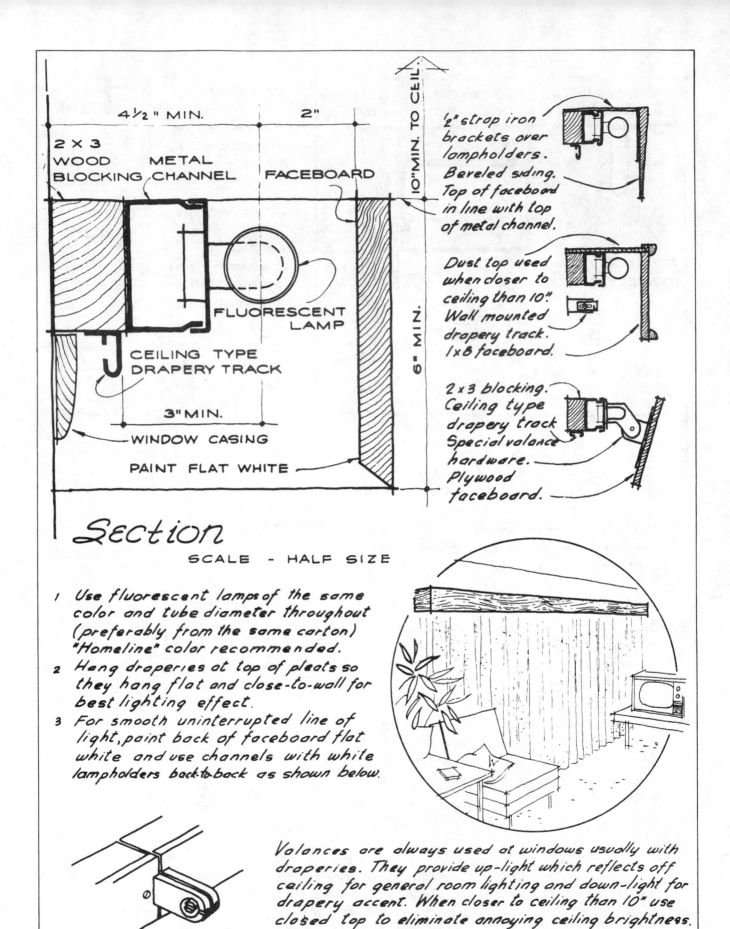

4½" MIN.   **2"**

2 × 3 WOOD BLOCKING   METAL CHANNEL   FACEBOARD

10" MIN. TO CEIL.

½" strap iron brackets over lampholders. Beveled siding. Top of faceboard in line with top of metal channel.

FLUORESCENT LAMP

CEILING TYPE DRAPERY TRACK

Dust top used when closer to ceiling than 10". Wall mounted drapery track. 1×8 faceboard.

6" MIN.

3" MIN.

WINDOW CASING

PAINT FLAT WHITE

2 × 3 blocking. Ceiling type drapery track. Special valance hardware. Plywood faceboard.

Section

SCALE - HALF SIZE

1 Use fluorescent lamps of the same color and tube diameter throughout (preferably from the same carton) "Homeline" color recommended.

2 Hang draperies at top of pleats so they hang flat and close-to-wall for best lighting effect.

3 For smooth uninterrupted line of light, paint back of faceboard flat white and use channels with white lampholders back-to-back as shown below.

Valances are always used at windows usually with draperies. They provide up-light which reflects off ceiling for general room lighting and down-light for drapery accent. When closer to ceiling than 10" use closed top to eliminate annoying ceiling brightness.

Customize a Venetian Blind with Fabric or Decoration

Custom-covering a blind to coordinate with the rest of your room is relatively easy, once you know how. Start with a new blind, or dress up an old one.

Tools and materials. Venetian blind; glue (if not using self-adhesive material); material for covering blind; razor blade.

Steps for covering a blind

1. Decide which side of the blind is viewed most often in the room; the top (convex) or bottom (concave). Plan to cover the side most often seen.

2. In choosing a blind for treatment, the 2" slat type is easiest, and blinds with almost invisible ladders (the supports that hold the slats in place) are most effective.

3. Measure length and confirm width of slats, to determine how much material is needed for covering. Count and number the slats, putting a piece of masking tape on the slat and a number on the tape.

4. If you have picked a material with a pattern, design, or illustration on it, remember that closed slats overlap. Be sure an important part of the design is not hidden under the overlap, and make a provision for it when cutting material. Allow extra yardage to make attractive overlaps.

5. Use the size of one slat as a pattern. Lay out your materials on a flat surface and mark off strips to cover slats. Number strips to correspond with numbers on slats.

6. With self-adhesive paper, just peel off backing and attach strips to slats.

7. For wallcovering or fabric, get appropriae adhesive from a paint or wallpaper store.

8. Test glue with fabric, to make sure that glue does not come through fabric to front surface. Thin, if necessary, and use thicker glue if it does come to fabric front.

9. Apply material to slat by dribbling a bead of glue down the center of the slat, then adding fabric. Edges can be tacked down later if initial bead does not spread evenly to edges.

10. With a sharp pointed knife or razor, cut out cord holes carefully. Follow the outline of the hole already in the metal slat.

Removing a blind

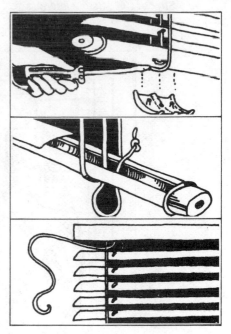

Give bottom ladder caps a little tug, then put the blade of a screwdriver next to the pin on the ladder cap and twist. That will pry the cap off. Do the same with other ladder caps.

Find the knot at the end of one lift cord. Untie it and pull it out of the bottom rail. Do the same with the other lift cords. Study the path the cord follows as it passes from slat to slat on alternating sides of each succeeding rung.

Reach to the top of the slats, grab the cords, and pull them up through the slats. Be careful not to pull them out of the head. The slats will now slide right out of the blind from either side. Mark each slat with a piece of masking tape along one side, and number if sequence is important in your covering with a pattern. Never reverse the slats end to end, since they won't line up precisely when you rehang them if you reverse them. (Illustration courtesy Levelor)

Steps to put a blind back up

1. Insert slats in proper sequence. After inserting about four slats, tilt blind closed to make sure slats are turned correctly.

2. Fuse ends of cord over a flame if necessary for easy threading

3. Re-thread cords through the holes. Start at the top with right cord and alternate it on left side of rung, then right side of rung, then left, and so on. For wide tapes, the rungs are offset alternately for each succeeding slat and the cord must pass straight along the center of the ladder to the bottom.

4. At bottom, bring the cord down through the center hole of the bottom rail, then up through the nearest hole. Knot the end. Pull all the slack from under and inside the bottom rail. Put the ladder caps back on.

5. If cords are unequal, move the knot you just tied or reknot the pull cord loop inside the tassel at the top.

Variation

• Paint a design directly on the blinds, or spray-paint them.

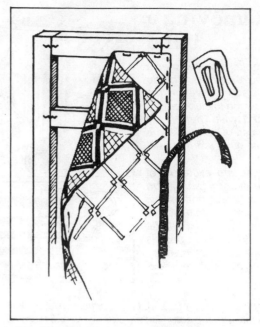

Attaching the fabric is easy with a staple gun. Trim hides the staples. (Courtesy of 1,001 Decorating Ideas)

EXCITING SCREENS AND DIVIDERS

Screens make dramatic additions to window treatments, and can be used to effectively separate areas of the living room. Just placing a screen in a corner may be enough to create architectural diversity. Dividers give each area a sense of privacy while allowing the eye to take full advantage of the spacial sweep of the entire room.

Fabric Panel Screen From Scratch

Once you have made a three-panel screen, you can add as many panels as you wish. This screen combines wood pieces with fabric panels.

Tools and materials. 1" x 2" lumber cut into six 6' lengths and twelve 12" lengths; white glue, corrugated nails; 1" finishing nails; sandpaper; paint; staple gun and staples; fabric; gimp; double-acting hinges.

Steps

1. Place each panel's wood parts on table or floor, with inner crosspieces at top and bottom and 8" from ends.

2. Glue joints and add corrugated nails front and back.

3. When glue is dry, toenail lumber together at ends with finishing nails.

Shirred curtains instead of panels give a more formal look. (Courtesy of 1,001 Decorating Ideas)

4. Sand frame smooth and paint.

5. Cut each fabric panel 1'' larger than screen opening all around, making sure to center pattern. Staple fabric in place in the back.

6. Glue gimp over staples and cut edges of fabric for a finished look from the back.

7. Attach double-acting hinges along sides (at the top, bottom, and middle of sides).

Variations

- Use shirred curtains instead of panels of fabric within the screen. Drill ⅜'' holes for curtain rods in uprights 1'' above and below braces, moving brace (inner cross piece) to chair-rail height. Use ½'' dowels as curtain rods. Cut fabric as you would for shirred curtains to fit openings in screen. Add finials to each top corner for a formal look.

- For window panels, make panels narrower, and eliminate the cross braces. A piano hinge is an elegant variation for attaching panels.

- Make solid plywood screens. Use ¾'' plywood 6'' high and 24'' wide for each panel. Wrap fabric to back and staple, or staple fabric in place in sides, then cover with gimp. Attach hinges last.

Flower enlargements in matching frames are an exciting three-dimensional decoration for a fabric–covered screen. (Courtesy of Richard W. Jones, FASID, for Eastman Kodak Co.)

Designer Michael Cannarozzi created this screen with fabric covering over plywood. Felt cutouts decorate the screen, simulating a sunrise. (Courtesy of 1,001 Decorating Ideas)

Make a Hanging Room Divider

A stationary hanging room divider is an architectural asset (plans courtesy Georgia-Pacific).

Tools and materials. Two panels ⅝'' x 4' x 8' T 1-11 plywood; four pieces 1'' x 4'' x 6' for outside frame; six pieces 1'' x 2'' x 6'; 2 pieces 1'' x 2'' x 8'; eye bolts; 3d and 8d finishing nails; white glue; surfacing putty.

Variations

- Use solid panels of plywood for the center of the divider. Paint or cover them with attractive fabric.
- Apply cork board to the back side of the divider as a bulletin board.

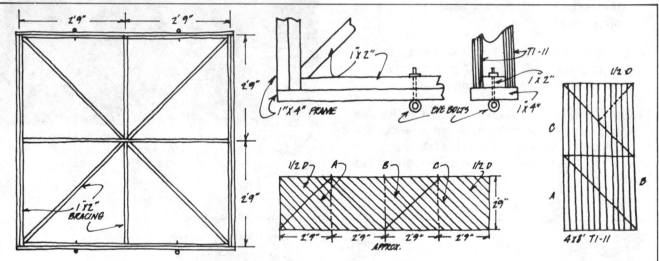

Hanging Room Divider

1. Mark the T 1-11 plywood panels carefully so they are mirror opposites. This will make the grooves match when assembled. Be sure to allow for saw kerf in cutting the adjoining pieces. Cut plywood panel diagonally as shown, then cut again into four 2'9'' squares.

2. Cut the 1 x 2 interior frame and braces and lay all parts out on the floor to be sure they fit before final assembly.

3. Apply glue and use corrugated fasteners on the corners to hold the interior frame square and in place when adding the plywood panels.

4. Assemble one side first, nailing and gluing sections of plywood to the 1 x 2 braces and interior frame. Use 3d finishing nails. Countersink and fill all nails used

in the panel, using wood dough or surfacing putty.

5. Spread padding such as several thicknesses of newspapers on the floor. Turn over assembled unit.

6. Cut 1 x 4s for outside frame for unit, making sure that top and bottom pieces are longer than 5½' because they will overlap the side frame parts as shown in drawing. Top and bottom 1 x 4s must each be one piece. Attach frame to paneling.

7. Install either tee nuts or eye bolts at top and bottom. If eye bolts are used, drill a small hole to prevent any splitting and to act as a guide before inserting them.

8. Glue and nail panels to the back side of unit, using 8d finishing nails.

TABLES CAN BE EASY TO MAKE

Once you have mastered furniture cube tables and a Parson's coffee table, you can vary the size to make tables to use throughout the house.

Parson's Coffee Table

The classic lines of this table make it beautiful, (plans courtesy Georgia-Pacific).

Tools and materials. One panel ¾'' x 4' x 8' Exterior medium density overlaid plywood; two pieces 1'' x 2'' x 40'' lumber for ledgers; two pieces 1'' x 2'' x 34½'' lumber for ledgers; ½ lb. of 1½'' finishing nails; saw; glue; wood filler; paint.

With these directions, the classic Parson's Coffee Table is easy to make. (Courtesy of Georgia-Pacific)

Steps

1. Cut out plywood pieces as indicated. Cut tabletop, two long sides and legs (F), two short sides and legs (A), two inside short sides and legs (D), two side parts (C), and four leg sides (E). Allow for saw kerfs between pieces.

2. Glue-nail the two 34½'' ledgers (B) to the inside of the leg pieces (A), ¾'' below upper edge as shown.

3. Assemble leg parts. Nail upright (E) to inside leg part (D); nail horizontal (C) to upright and inside leg part; nail short outside leg (A) to upright (E) and (C). Glue where necessary.

4. Slide these units inside long side (F) pieces and glue/nail.

5. Fit 40'' ledgers between the plywood legs as shown, and glue/nail ¾'' below upper edge of the table.

6. Glue/nail 34½'' x 46½'' plywood tabletop into assembled frame. Fill all nail holes and exposed edges with wood filler. Sand and paint as desired.

Variations

- Cover the table with fabric, wallcovering, or any manner of creative decoration.
- Alter the size to make Parson's tables for many uses.

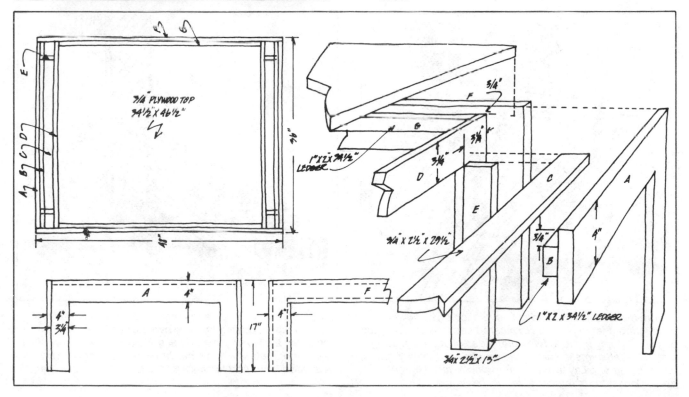

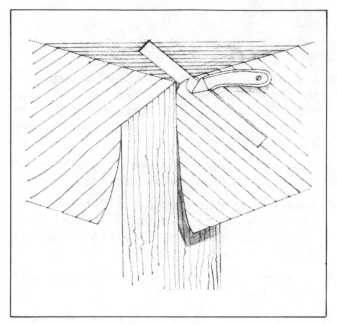

1. Prime raw wood table for a good hold; allow to dry. Center fabric on top, allowing enough to lap 1" to underside of apron. Secure with thumbtacks or pins. Mix paste, roll back fabric halfway, and apply paste to half of tabletop surface. Pat fabric in place and repeat on other half of table. Apply paste to apron and pat down fabric. While paste is still wet, use a metal straight edge and mat knife to miter corners. Peel away fabric along miters, then cut remainder with knife. Turn table on its back and roll paste to underside and inside of apron. Fold fabric to inside and pat smoothly into place.

COVERING A PARSON'S TABLE WITH FABRIC

Follow these basic steps (from *1,001 Decorating Ideas*).

Tools and materials. Fabric with fairly close weave; thumbtacks or push pins; vinyl wallpaper paste or spray adhesive; 3" roller; roller pan; metal straight-edge; razor/knife; furniture glides.

Three Tables in a Compact Cube

These occasional tables work at the end of a sofa or anywhere (plans courtesy of Georgia-Pacific).

Tools and materials. Two panels ¾" x 4' x 8' Interior grade plywood; two pieces 2" x 2" x 10' lumber; white glue; wood putty; 6d nails; sealer; fine sandpaper; semi-gloss or gloss enamel or spray paint.

Variations

• Use different colors for each table, or a mono-chromatic selection.
• Cover with interesting materials such as those suggested for Parson's table.

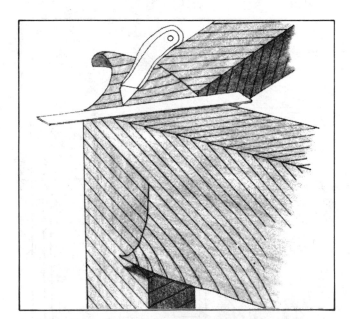

2. Turn table on its side and cut covers for legs, allowing a ½" overlap. Match patterns to mitered sections as nearly as possible. Apply paste to two outer sides of each leg, using a small brush to make sure paste reaches all the way into the mitered corners. Lay fabric overlapping mitered corners; press front sides of leg cover fabric into place.

3. Apply paste to inside surfaces of legs. Press rest of leg cover in place, adding paste to overlapped seam. Pin to hold. Trim away excess fabric at bottom with scissors. Work paste under fabric with a small brush at feet if necessary for a good hold. Add furniture glides to bottom of each leg.

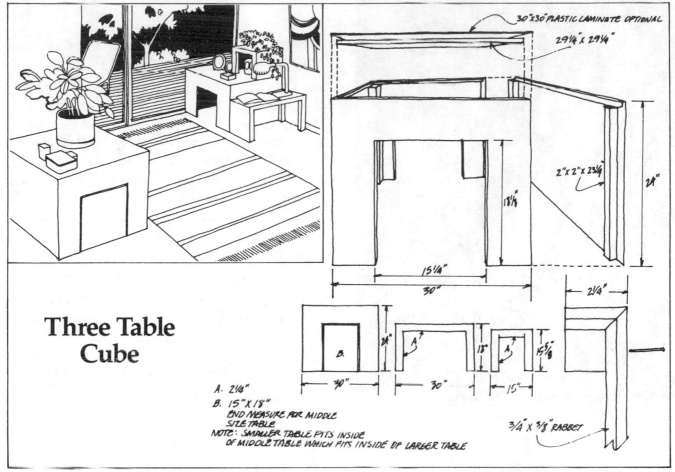

Three Table Cube

30"x30" PLASTIC LAMINATE OPTIONAL

29¼" X 29¼"

2"x 2"x 23¼"

24"

18⅛"

15¼"

30"

2¼"

24"

A"

18"

A"

15⅝"

B.

30"

30"

15"

¾" X ⅜" RABBET

A. 2¼"
B. 15" X 18"
END MEASURE FOR MIDDLE
SIZE TABLE
NOTE: SMALLER TABLE FITS INSIDE
OF MIDDLE TABLE WHICH FITS INSIDE OF LARGER TABLE

1. Allowing for your saw kerf, cut pieces for first table of ¾" plywood. Cut four pieces 24" x 30", and one piece measuring 29¼" square.
2. Miter all 24" sides and cut a rabbet ¾" deep along 30" upper edge.
3. Mark two sides for openings measuring 15¼" wide by 18⅛" high on center. Drill a ¼" hole in the two inside corners to start cutting.
4. Glue/nail cut-to-length 2 x 2s to inside along miter where corner will be and set aside to dry.
5. Glue/nail four sides together, making sure two opening pieces are opposite one another. Clamp if necessary and allow to dry. Glue/nail top into place.
6. To finish, fill with wood putty, and sand smooth.
7. To make smaller tables, use measure given and follow the same procedures.

MAKE ACCESSORY PILLOWS

You can stuff your own pillows with batting or buy ready-made pillows to cover. Use exciting fabrics to make a collection of coordinated pillows, and experiment by using piping to outline pillow edges, or by creating a floppy border up to 2" deep by cutting cover larger and topstitching to the wider width for the border.

Make Harem Pillows for Sitting on the Floor

Harem pillow designs are good for sitting on the floor because they are puffy and look amply stuffed. The seam around the sides of each pillow is pulled in, and corners are gathered and rounded. Of course, smaller versions are fine for accessory pillows. Designer sheets are ideal for making matched or mix-matched sets of harem pillows (directions from Springmaid Fashions).

Stuffed harem pillows can be used to co-ordinate with other furniture in the room. (Courtesy of Simmons)

Tools and materials. Attractive cording; pillow stuffing (foam or polyester batting); twin flat sheet.

Steps

1. Cut two squares of fabric 36'' x 36''. Turn right sides together, and sew around all four sides, rounding corners and leaving an 8'' opening centered on one side.

2. Trim seam to ¼'', turn right side out, and press edge flat.

3. Sew around sides ⅝'' in from edge (through both layers), except for opening. Push cord through this casing with a big safety pin. Stuff pillow.

4. Pin the opening shut; hand sew it closed.

5. Pull the cord to make the pillow firm and adjust gathers so that they are at corners. Tie the cord in front and knot ends.

Pillows are the softening elements in this fabric-filled room that reflects the Golden Oak styles of the turn of the century. Velcro-closing pillows fill the window seat as well as wicker furniture. (Furniture and fabric from Montgomery Ward)

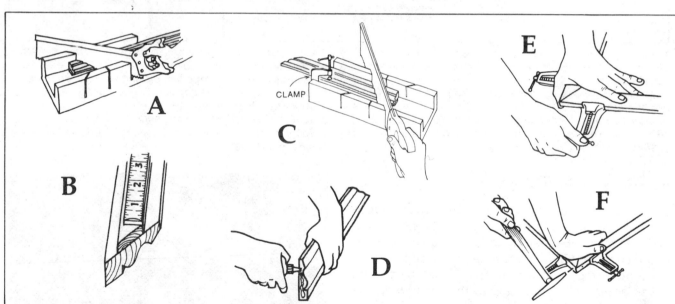

Glue molding strips that will make your complete frame. Clamp or weight until glue has set; allow to dry thoroughly. Saw off end of molding at 45 degree angle. Carefully measure bottom edge of picture, add ⅛'' to this measure and transfer measurement to molding. (Cut long side first.) Start from edge of miter and mark the above length. Cut a 45 degree miter at opposite angle from one you've just cut, to make the bottom section of the picture frame. Use this section to make an identical piece for the top of the frame.

Measure for the shorter side of the picture and cut a piece of molding this length, not forgetting to add the extra ⅛''. Measure the second side from the one just completed.

To assemble the frame, take one side piece and the bottom piece and coat the ends to be joined with glue, then place in corner clamp. When corner is aligned just right, tighten clamp to exert sufficient pressure to hold pieces rigidly enough so you can nail the corner together.

Drive two or more brads through the corner from each side, allowing the heads of the brads to protrude slightly.

Check that the frame is square by measuring the diagonals, which should be equal. A slight push on the long diagonal will square up your frame. Carefully finish driving brads with a small nail set so that heads are about 1/16'' below surface of frame.

MAKE YOUR OWN PICTURE FRAMES

By combining molding, you can customize your own picture frames and save money in the process. There are more than 250 molding patterns and 400 sizes to choose from—enough to afford variety throughout any house. These instructions and illustrations are from the Western Wood Moulding and Millwork Producers.

Tools and materials. Molding; light hammer; small nail set; ruler; fine-toothed saw; small nails; corner fasteners; pencil; fine sandpaper; brads; glue. Some type of miter box is necessary to make 45 degree corner cut. One corner clamp is necessary, while four is most convenient.

Variations

• Paint frames, or use a combination of paint and natural or stained frame. Stained frames are

finished just like natural frames after stain is applied.

• Texturize the frame with paint. Start with a coat of warm or cool gray heavy-bodied paint such as latex type. Before this paint sets, texture surface by using a sponge, making lines with a comb, etc. When dry, this surface is colored with thin paint applied with a cloth. Choose colors that will enhance the beauty of the painting to be displayed. Finish when dry with a light coat of good paste wax.

• Use these pointers in matching your frame to the artwork: black and white usually take a narrow frame; pencil drawings, watercolors, and pastels are better matted and under glass; oils are almost always framed without glass; subjects with a sense of depth can use a deep frame; flat or abstract subject matter looks well with a narrow strip frame; all the above are merely suggestions—there are no rules.

LIGHTING YOU CAN DESIGN

Lighting is one of the crucial elements in setting the mood of a room. Even if you plan to buy all your lighting fixtures, start with your personal plan for their correct placement, size, scale, and relationship to one another. You also can make some lighting fixtures yourself. Keep abreast of the new developments in both lighting fixtures and bulbs. New breakthroughs are constantly being made in energy saving, design, and particular application to a specific job.

Here are some general guidelines for buying and making your own lighting fixtures. Use them for lighting throughout the house (suggestions from General Electric).

General Lighting Recommendations

Plan your total lighting arrangement. You will need: general or fill-in lighting for low level of light throughout the area—usually provided by ceiling fixtures, lighted valances or wall brackets, groupings of open-top portable lamps, or a combination of these; local or functional lighting, usually portable lamps or built-in fixtures for specific task lighting—for sewing, musical score reading, casual reading, card playing, knitting, etc.; accent or decorative lighting, which includes wall washers, high-hat recessed downlights, candle-

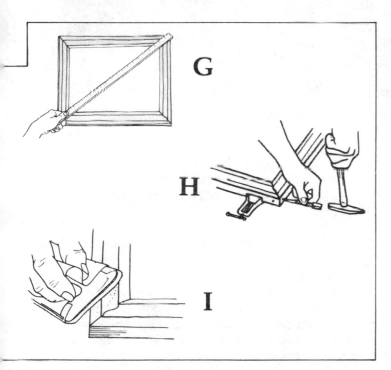

G

H

I

A strip of wood tacked onto back of frame will hold the square until glue dries. Fill nail holes with a little wood putty or fine sawdust (from cutting the frame) mixed with glue. If the frame is of wide molding, add a corner fastener to further strengthen the joint. Follow same procedure on the other three corners.

To finish, sand lightly. Any number of finishes are handsome, including leaving frame natural with protections of three coats of shellac with light sanding in between. Then surface is coated with paste wax and buffed.

Track lighting can turn an ordinary wall into a miniature gallery. Adjustable white lamp-holders can be focussed to best light each painting. (Courtesy of Halo Power Trac lighting)

light simulating chandeliers, and all lighting that creates a focal point or adds a personal and distinctive touch.

Ceiling-mounted fixtures. These should have only half the surface brightness of fixtures in utility areas, because they are readily seen from any point in a room. Similarly, pendant fixtures should have half the surface brightness of ceiling-mounted fixtures. These fixtures should be attractive, not glaring. Many small-diameter pendant fixtures should have 25 watts or less for comfortable viewing.

Directional downlights. Use to light up dining or game tables by placing diagonally from each corner about 2' out. Avoid placing them directly over any seating locations. Dimmers enable you to control light levels for greatest effect and comfort.

This full-range dimmer installs as easily as a conventional switch. (Courtesy of Leviton Manufacturing Co.)

Portable lamps. These spread their light over a limited area, about 40 to 50 square feet, and usually serve as lighting for only one individual's activities. To make your lamps work, follow these general suggestions:

1. base height—total height from floor to lower edge of shade (including table height) should equal eye height from floor (from 38" to 42") for person seated in a lounge chair;

2. bulb size—use three-way or regular bulbs with a minimum of 150 watts for reading (three-way is preferred as it can be turned on low when not needed for reading);

3. under-shade features—socket should be in line with bottom edge of shade, and soft-white bulbs are preferred (diffusers may be desirable for reading lamps and directional control devices that reflect light coming below shade can expand quantity of light to far side of a desk or work area);

4. shade size and shape—open tops are recommended, although shallower shades need a shield or louver in the top so light does not glare in your eyes when you stand (deeper shades need extra-long harps or recessed top fitting—minimum dimension for practicality is a 16" bottom);

5. shade material for reading lamps—moderately translucent is preferred to solidly opaque, i.e., moderate-transmission white vinyl or parchment laminated to fabric, or white-lined fabric, if fairly dense (dense or opaque shades are best only when room is very dramatic with very dark walls);

6. shade colors—avoid strong or dark colors on outside unless material is opaque, and be sure that inside is white or near white, never shiny. All shades in the same room should have similar brightness for cohesion. Colored linings tint the light; foil linings reflect the light meagerly and with harshness.

Planning specific placements. A senior table lamp placed in the back corner of a corner table will probably not provide sufficient lighting for more than one reader seated near it. It would be best to move the lamp to one side to provide good reading for at least one seat. In this case, it should be about 16" back from where book is held, and no more than 20" to the side. If the lamp is very tall, place it in the floor lamp position. This is with the base or shaft in line with the shoulder for low floor lamps. A tall standing lamp (43" to 49" base to shade) should be placed 15" left or right of book center and 26" back. Wall lamps are placed with shade center in line with shoulder and 20" left or right of book center. If wall lamp is substantially behind the shoulder, raise and center 15" to side with lower shade edge 47" to 49".

Install Track Lighting

Steps for installing track lighting are covered in the preceding chapter on entrances and exits. You may install track lighting horizontally on ceiling, rather than vertically on walls. Do not overlook the possibilities of installing track lighting in "U" and "L" shapes or any other ways, in addition to the popular straight line applications.

Make Your Own Table Lamps

Virtually any material can be used for a table lamp. You will need to find a source for lampmaking materials, which may be a local lampmaking specialty shop. Shades are available ready-made, and easily can be personalized by adding your own outer covering. Once you have made your first lamp, you can use the same knowledge to create many more. Most are constructed like Dagwood sandwiches on a stick.

Making a lamp is easy with this cork-based switch that comes in a kit. Just insert it in a bottle top. (Courtesy of Leviton Manufacturing Co.)

Light up your jelly beans or anything else with this do-it-yourself lamp kit. The canister base, push-through socket, and square–cut ribbon trim shade plus glass ball finial are all included. The lamp is 18" high. You add your own jelly beans. (Courtesy of Hilo Stiner)

Tools and materials. A ⅜" lamp pipe threaded at both ends, long enough to accommodate base object; platform made of wood or plastic; object to become lamp base, such as a jar, vase, basket, or wood cube; feet of knobs or upholstery tacks to elevate base if base does not come with feet; finial; harp; detachable harp base; vase cap for round opening; ½" threaded nipple; coupling; three locknuts; three-way socket with screw terminals; lamp cord; electrical plug.

Steps

1. Choose object for the base. Decide on desirable overall height of lamp, and select a base tall enough to bring assembled lamp to that height.

2. Finish base if needed. Drill hole for the pipe with ⅜" bit, making sure hole is centered and truly vertical. Counterbore wood base underneath for insertion of locknut. Drill a horizontal rabbet or hole for cord to go to edge of lamp. (Or add small feet to base so that cord merely rests underneath.)

3. Drill hole (or have one drilled) in jar or vase ⅜", centered.

4. Insert pipe through vase and wood base, securing it underneath with locknut.

5. Attach locknut at top of vase, then attach vase cap. Add coupling and make sure it is secure. Base part is complete.

6. Work ½" threaded nipple into coupling. Add detachable harp base. Secure with a locknut. Add socket base.

7. Insert lamp cord through pipe, etc. Make an underwriter's knot and attach wires to screw terminals. Work cord down so that it is flush with socket base, and socket is securely into base. Cover with cardboard insulation and outer metal sheath.

8. Run cord along rabbet or through horizontal opening at base. Add electrical plug.

9. Top with harp, shade, and finial, have lamp checked by a licensed electrician, add a bulb, and that's it.

Variations

• Use any kind of material for a base that comes to mind. Investigate rosewood vase bases as ready-made, elegant platforms for lampmaking.

• Use a wood platform with a bent pipe so that your chosen object need not be drilled, but can still be displayed below the lampshade. Think carefully before drilling holes in antiques. You render them far less valuable with lampmaking holes, in most cases.

• Dress up a plain shade to adorn your new lamp with trim that color coordinates with the base. Attach to any ready-made shade with a bead of white glue.

• Buy an especially made see-through lamp base to hold your favorite collections. Good collection examples are shells, rocks, potpourri, even jelly beans.

A fabulous grand entrance is created with the use of diagonal cedar planks on massive double doors. Tomato-red paint sets off the entry area for an unusual effect. Design for a Kingsberry home by Evan Frances, ASID, and J. Christopher Jones. (Photo courtesy of 1001 Decorating Ideas Magazine)

Coordinated screens set off the window in this room giving it a more interesting shape, and emphasizing its importance. "Pagoda" wallcovering from Stauffer Chemical Co. was used in the design by Alan Scruggs, ASID.

The paneled wall and fireplace mantel work give this room its focus. Use of paneling and molding from the local store created the traditional look of priceless restored architectural detailing. Traditional Ethan Allen furnishings are naturally grouped to dramatize the hearth. (Photo courtesy of Ethan Allen)

Conventional paneling can be worked diagonally to create attractive backgrounds. It features a contemporary arched doorway with cut-outs. The furniture is knock-down, but with a substantial look, from James David Incorporated.

◄ *Stunning rosewood reproduction paneling by Masonite and track lighting enclosed in an overhead cornice give this room its style. It is installed in a Kingsberry home, designed for the do-it-yourselfer. Design by Evan Frances, ASID, and J. Christopher Jones. (Photo courtesy of 1001 Decorating Ideas Magazine)*

By night, Duro-Lite's Vita-Lite Power Twist fluorescents installed behind decorative louvers provide "indoor sunshine" to nourish this hanging garden. (Photo courtesy of Duro-Lite Lamps Inc.)

Contrasting but coordinated fabric and wallcovering are used to create this garden effect. Screens rather than draperies beside the windows give a modern look. Simple easy-to-make cubes painted white show off both plants and sculpture. (Photo courtesy of Contac, from "Great News" Wallcoverings)

Velcro closing pillows take their color cues from the floral wallcovering used in this living room. Gloria Vanderbilt design wallcovering is from James Seeman Studios, Inc.

Paint and tape transform an ordinary foyer when used to create tromphe l'oeil panels. (Photo courtesy 1001 Decorating Ideas)

Shirred fabrics soften the effect of walls and are played against the deep tone of paint used on every other wall surface. A Parson's table is covered with leather and upholsterer's tacks. Note the subtle side shelf that doubles as a tabletop beside the hearth. All lamps are traditionally styled by Stiffel. All fabrics by P. Kaufmann, and carpeting as well, are treated with "Scotchgard" Protector. Furniture is courtesy of Classic Leather & Vanguard.

Mirrors set off the dining area of this living room, and give the look of expanded space at the same time. These are simply installed mirror tiles, on screens as well as walls. (Photo courtesy of 1001 Decorating Ideas Magazine)

3
Kitchen Schemes

The kitchen is the most expensive room in many homes. It is the scene of many major and costly remodeling changes. Relatively simple and inexpensive alterations, however, can well bring your kitchen into the new age. Entire books can be written about kitchen planning, and have been. For major undertakings, you may want to refer to *Successful Kitchens* by Patrick Galvin, or your local contractor.

Here are some tips from the editors of *1,001 Decorating Ideas* for deciding which route to take in planning your kitchen remodeling.

- Determine why you're remodeling—Sorting "needs" from "wants" helps eliminate pie-in-the-sky ideas. For example, if you're aiming for a different "ambience," new appliances may be necessary. If it's greater convenience you need, appliances you already own may be repositioned to save you steps.

- Plan—Planning will help you avoid costly oversights. Be professional—use floor plans, drawings, and swatches of wallcovering and paints.

- Avoid structural changes—Changing walls, adding floor space, exposing beams, etc., costs more than just using existing space in new ways. Professional designers often "pay their own way" by creating cost-cutting plans.

- Use existing plumbing and electrical lines—Rerouting these lines is costly. Change them only when increased convenience justifies the expense.

- Consider doing some things yourself—Many contractors will do major structural work and leave the finishing (like papering, painting, paneling a wall, or installing an acoustical tile ceiling) to handy homeowners. Installing cabinets can mean a big savings; so can laying your own flooring. Discuss the possibilities with your contractor.

REFINISHING CABINETS

If the wood is still in good shape, you can refinish rather than replace your cabinet doors and drawers. Many companies specialize in this, and can offer reasonable prices such as $10 per door, which includes the additional built-in cabinet area as well. Or you can tackle the job yourself.

Refinishing kitchen woodwork is not an especially complicated or expensive project to do yourself, but be prepared for it to take quite a while, and to mess up your kitchen in the meantime. If at all possible get several people working on the detachable parts—doors and drawers—to cut down the amount of sanding and hours and sweat.

Tools and materials. Lots of newspaper on which to do your varnish removing and staining; rubber gloves; a scraper, about 3" wide with a sharp, flat edge; a brush to apply the varnish remover; fine sandpaper; rags to apply the stain; a brush to apply the final coat of varnish or lacquer.

Steps

1. Remove the doors from the hinges and then remove the hardware (knob pulls; leave hinges on doors). This is important to avoid leaving small patches on the edges of the door.

2. Lay the door or drawer down on several sheets of newspaper; or, if doing the woodwork, place newspapers along the floor. Always use rubber gloves. Brush on the varnish remover, making sure to cover all surfaces on the side facing up. Let sit about 10 minutes, and with a smooth motion scrape off the old varnish. It will peel off in clumps, but might require two or three coats to get all the way down to the wood at all points. Turn the door over and do the second side.

3. Rub with solvent to get any remaining varnish out of grooves.

◀ *Use photographic blow-ups of vegetables and fruit to cover kitchen cabinet doors. Adhere the prints directly to wooden doors, then cover them with a protective finish. Any series of photographs will do, so long as they follow a theme. (Designed by Richard W. Jones, FASID, for Eastman Kodak Company)*

▼ *Replace upper cabinet doors with shutter doors with fabric inserts to match fabric used in other areas of the kitchen. Use three colors of paint; one for panel centers, one for molding trim, and one for cabinets and door outer edges. Paint molding before attaching, and touch-up once it is attached where necessary. Use the same molding treatment to customize and coordinate other kitchen elements, such as built-in window seat with storage beneath. (Photo courtesy of Armstrong)*

Modernize painted plain cabinets by adding panels of wallcovering. Paint cabinets first, then cut out round-cornered panels of ¼" plywood. Fill and sand plywood edges and paint the same color as cabinets. Apply wallcovering to panels. Attach panels to doors with paneling adhesive. ("Bonny Plaid" vinyl laminate wallcovering by James Seeman Studios)
▼

Use molding to outline decorative panels on cabinet doors. ▶
Bamboo-patterned wood half-round molding can outline
doors, cornice, soffits, and create a see-through grille-
archway into a separate eating area. Use two moldings side
by side on both door and cabinet sides. The pattern created is
sufficiently strong that units can be painted the same color
and still have visual impact. (Bamboo-patterned Thomasville
Furniture; Designer Solarian flooring from Armstrong)

Keep your cabinets clean-lined, but paint them a bright ▼
new favorite color. Add pattern to the kitchen by using tile
stick-ons to dress up the splash-plate area. Follow through
with stick-ons to decorate a windowshade valance. (Stick-
ons from Contact)

Use wallcovering inserts inside molding-created panels on
door fronts. Paint the cabinets and doors first, then attach and
paint molding. When thoroughly dry, add wallcovering inserts, cutting away from molding with a sharp razor or knife.
An alternative method is to outline molding inside dimensions
on doors and cut wallcovering to overlap slightly. Molding
then can be attached over wallcovering edges to hide them.
(Designer Solarian Flooring from Armstrong)
▼

4. Sand evenly and firmly with fine sandpaper.

5. Apply stain with long, brushing movements using rags. Make sure the stain has been well stirred, and that you have allowed enough time for the solvent, used to wash down the wood, to evaporate. Make the first staining a "wet" layer—heavy and dark. Let sit about ten to fifteen minutes, and then wipe off with a soft absorbent cloth, again with even strokes. Then wait an hour. Apply a second coat, but not as heavy, working it until you get approximately the shade desired. Wipe again after ten minutes. If it still is not dark enough, apply a light final coat to darken with no excess to wipe off. Let sit 24 hours or more before applying lacquer or varnish.

6. To get a glossy finish, apply two or three coats of varnish or lacquer (follow directions on the can). To get a smooth, satiny finish, sand down the first coat after it has dried completely (fine sandpaper again), and then apply a second coat; sand again once completely dry and hard (or just use "satin" varnish).

Finishing Touches

Remember to include your appliances in the refinishing/recovering scheme of things. Refrigerators, freezers, and dishwashers can be customized to match your general paint job or for wallcovering applications. Check for special paints and materials that lend themselves to being used on appliance surfaces.

Use new hardware to spice up cabinets. The hardware alone can change a colonial look to modern, or a Mediterranean to rustic early American. Knobs and pulls usually are metal and can be finished in an entire range of enamel colors or metal finishes, such as brass, bronze, brushed chrome, or antique pewter. Some are ceramic or plastic. They are available from kitchen centers in an equally broad range of designs.

INSTALLING KITCHEN CABINETS

In case the old cabinets just won't do, here are the methods for installing new ones. Proper installation is the most important factor in the convenience, wear, and good looks of your cabinets. The cheapest cabinets available give better service when installed properly than expensive cabinets that are poorly installed. Cabinets must be installed level, plumb, and true. With this in mind. you may want to make the

creative decisions on types of cabinets, and turn the installation over to a professional. If not, steps to follow on pages 61 and 62, should enable the handy person to begin. For further details, see *Successful Kitchens*, by Patrick Galvin.

COUNTERTOPS

Countertops are unsung heroes. They resist heat, freezing cold, countless washings, and stain from everything, e.g., from peanut butter and jelly, and potting soil. They stay in one piece no matter how overladen, and are generally overlooked.

In the long run, it is simply not a good investment to put in a countertop that is not highly durable. This means one of the favorite materials or a combination of favorites is best. Top choices include high-pressure laminates (such as Formica) of a proper thickness (1/16"), laminated hardwood such as butcherblock or tempered glass ceramic for cutting operations, and heat resisters, such as ceramic tile. Alternates are stainless steel and marble.

Plastic Laminated Countertops

Plastic laminated countertops are by far the most popular, with tile countertops a favorite in the Southwest. Since you cannot laminate or make the plastic laminated top yourself, concentrate on making sure that your specifications and quality pointers to the fabricator are accurate and complete. Here are some guidelines.

Types of tops. Tops are either self-edged or postformed. Self-edged tops are flat and have a square front and edging that is a separate piece of the same material. Hence the name. The backsplash is a separate unit of the same material with a square inside corner that is attached at the shop before delivery. Usually the backsplash is 4", but this type of top can rise all the way to the bottoms of the wall cabinets or to any height you desire, such as up to the window apron.

Postformed tops present one clean sweep of plastic surface from the bottom of the front edge to the top of the backsplash. Because of limitations in its fabrication, high backsplashes are not possible with postformed tops.

Thickness. Fabricators usually use ¾" particleboard as a corestock. The finished product must be at least that thickness, and it might vary up to 1 ¾", but this is extravagant in most cases and the extra

Installing Your Cabinet

1

Cabinets must be attached to studs for full support. Studs are usually located 16 inches on center. Locate studs with stud finder, tapping with hammer or nail driven through plaster at height that will be hidden by cabinets. Cabinets must always be attached to walls with screws. Never use nails!

2

Cabinets must be installed perfectly level — from a standpoint of function as well as appearance. Find the highest point of floor with the use of a level.

3

Using a level or straightedge, find the high spots on the wall on whcih cabinets are to be hung. Some high spots can be removed by sanding. Otherwise, it will be necessary to "shim" to provide a level and plumb installation.

4

Using the highest point on the floor, measure up the wall to a height of 84 inches. This height, 84 inches, is the top height of wall cabinets, oven and broom cabinets.

5

On the walls where cabinets are to be installed, remove baseboard and chair rail. This is required for a flush fit.

6

Start your installation in one corner. First assemble the base corner unit, then adding one unit on each side of the corner unit. This — as a unit — can be installed in position. Additional cabinets are then added to each side as required.

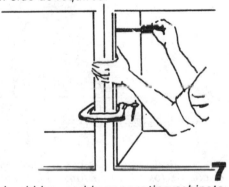

7

"C" clamps should be used in connecting cabinets together to obtain proper alignment. Drill 2 or 3 holes through ½ inch end panels. Holes should be drilled through to adjoining cabinet. Secure T-nut and secure with 1½ inch bolt. Draw up snugly. If you prefer you may drill through side of front frame as well as "lead hole" into abutting cabinet, insert screws and draw up snugly.

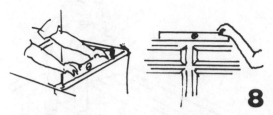

8

Each cabinet — as it is installed to the wall — should be checked front to back and also across the front edge with a level. Be certain that the front frame is plumb. If necessary, use shims to level the cabinets. Base cabinets should be attached with screws into wall studs. For additional support and to prevent back rail from "bowing," insert block between cabinet back and wall. After bases are installed cover toe kick area with material that is provided.

9

Attach countertop on base cabinets. After installation, cover countertops with cartons to prevent damage while completing installation.

10

Wall cabinets should then be installed, beginning with a corner unit as described in step #6. Screw through hanging strips built into backs of cabinets at both top and bottom. Place them ¾ inch below top and ¾ inch above bottom shelf from inside of cabinet. Adjust only loosely at first so that final adjustments can be made.

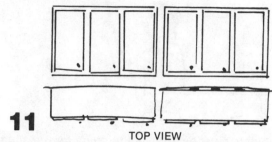

11

TOP VIEW

Wall cabinets should be checked with level on cabinet front, sides, and bottom to insure that cabinets are plumb and level. It might be necessary to shim at wall and between cabinets to correct for uneven walls or floors. After cabinets and doors are perfectly aligned, tighten all screws.

This sequence is from the installation manual of Kitchen Kompact, a giant of the industry.

Problem Doors

There are very few "perfect" conditions where floors and walls are exactly level and plumb. Therefore, it is necessary to correct this by proper "shimming" so that the cabinet is not racked or twisted and so that cabinet doors are properly aligned.

The top left hand corner is pulled into a low spot on wall. A shim is needed between cabinet and wall at this point.

Before: Doors are out of line. Cabinet is racked.

TOP VIEW

Detailed line reveals top edge of cabinet slightly out of line.

Use level to see if cabinet face is plumb on both edges. Same condition exists if lower right hand corner of cabinet is against a high spot on wall. Remove the high spot (by sanding) or shim other three corners.

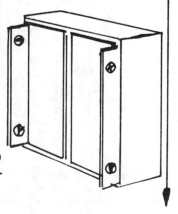

After: Doors are aligned properly. Cabinet is plumb and level.

SHIM
TOP VIEW

Tiles transform this range/barbecue unit, giving a colorful custom look in a rich Primitive Raven black. Tiles are 4″ x 8″. (Photo courtesy of American Olean)

thickness is not needed. Depth from the front to rear would be 24″ or 25″, enough to extend a minimum of ⅛″ or a maximum of ½″ over the cabinets beneath, (figures from the standards of the National Association of Plastic Fabricators).

Support.   Regular kitchen countertops properly attached to base cabinets need no backing sheet for dimensional stability. The structure itself will prevent warping. But peninsulas that extend several feet out from the base cabinets must have backing sheets.

Relationship to walls.   Tops that must be positioned tightly between walls must be ¼″ to ⅜″ short. Otherwise, a top that measures the same as the between-walls dimension will not go into position.

Out-of-square walls.   Most walls are not square. To measure and compensate for this, kitchen specialists use a simple formula: $3' + 4' = 5'$. To use it, measure two walls from the corner where they meet. Measure the base wall to a point 3′ from the corner and mark the point. Then measure along the side wall and mark a point 4′ from the corner. Now measure the distance between the two points. It should be 5′. If it measures less than 5′, the side wall is coming in. If it measures more than 5 feet, the side wall is going out. Tell the precise measurements to the fabricator so he can allow for them and make the top fit.

Seaming.   Improper placing of laminate seams can cause cracks. When seams are mitered from front to back in corners, it avoids stresses that come with no miter. In addition, all corners of sink or range cutouts should be radiused. Square corners in these places tend to crack.

Tiled Countertops

The step-by-step illustrations from American Olean Tile show how you can add a tile surface over a conventional plastic laminated top. This is one way of revamping a countertop that is marred beyond repair.

Tools and materials.   Tile, including trim tile; AO 1800 solvent type I adhesive; notched trowel; nippers; tile cutter's dry grout; rubberfaced groutmaster trowel; wood striking tool; wet sponge; cloth.

63

Installing A Tile Countertop

(The following illustrations are courtesy of American Olean Tile)

1. Here is how the countertop looked before it was covered to match the new color scheme. Note that the sink has a lip which overlaps the counter.

2. The sink and other elements that are set into the countertop are removed. Then trim tile is laid out, starting at corners where full tiles are desirable. Then the necessary cuts are calculated in the middle of the counter.

3. AO 1800, a solvent type I adhesive, is spread with a notched trowel. It is suitable for application of ceramic tile over vitreous surfaces such as concrete, exterior grade plywood, plastic laminate, terrazzo, and existing ceramic tile.

4. Trim pieces, S-4449, are installed in adhesive with ¼" overhang.

5. Nippers are used to shape tiles to contour of opening.

6. Additional tile is installed. Cuts are made as necessary to conform to sink area.

7. One course of trim is placed on the backsplash with ¼" projection above existing laminate to permit overlap for 1" cut piece which will be applied later.

8. 1" wide strips for the top edge of the backsplash can be easily made with a simple cutter. Scoring is shown here. Tile is broken cleanly by exerting pressure with cutter on both sides of scored line.

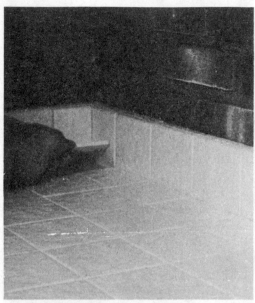

◄Tile is installed at top of back-splash. Pieces of trim are cut and applied to the apron at front of counter in a similar fashion. These pieces will adhere better if adhesive is permitted to "set-up" for a few minutes. Adhesives are then applied to field of countertop, and those tiles are applied. Last, the corner piece is installed.

When all tile is installed but ▶ not grouted, sink and range top are put temporarily into position to check fit.

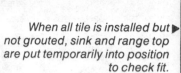

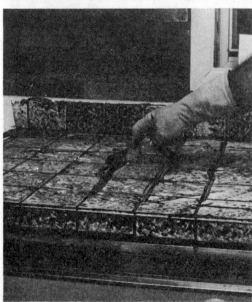

◄Dry grout is put into a pail and mixed with water. (In this case a dark brown, non-sanded grout is used, one suitable for narrow seams.) It is spread with a rubber-faced groutmaster trowel. Grouting should be done the day following installation to permit adhesive to dry. Joints are then leveled with a tool (preferably wood or plastic) to compact the grout in the joints.

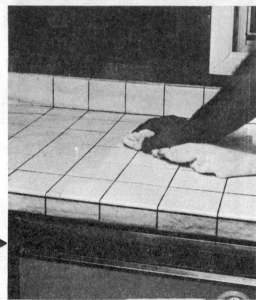

Excess grout is taken from ▶ surface of tile with a wet sponge and then surface is polished with a clean, dry cloth.

Peninsulas make popular snack counters. One such as this that is the same height as the counter calls for stool chairs, higher than normal seating. (Courtesy of Wallcovering Industry Bureau)

A clever country touch is added to this kitchen by joining a conventional table as the peninsula. Surface matches the countertop, while leaf extends for additional seating. (Photo courtesy of Azrock Vinyl)

EFFICIENT EATING AREAS

A place for a snack or light meal, integrated into your kitchen design, is a convenience that makes an ordinary kitchen highly congenial. Even with a full table in the kitchen, clean-ups are easiest when small snacks are served on an easily cleaned counter. Most counters can double as the food planning area, and can be built with the addition of a space for recipe books.

Convenient Dimensions

Here are measurements to consider in planning your eating area. You may have to adapt these suggestions to suit your space.

Elbow room. Allow 20" to 24" of elbow room for each place setting, side to side. Depth for snacks and light meals is 15". For dinners (when more elements such as serving dishes are also used on the surface), allow 24" of depth.

Height for an island or peninsula. The standard is 36", with 12" to 18" for knee space underneath, depending on seating. Remember that you will need high stools or chairs to suit the standard height.

Snack bar height. This can drop to 30". If you still have small children in the house, the lower height is safest as well as most convenient for them.

Space behind chairs. A minimum of 32" is needed for ease in pulling out and sitting on chairs. To edge past a seated person, 36" is necessary.

Snack areas. These look best when seating can be tucked underneath when not in use, perhaps with merely the backs showing.

Dining area. Remember to consider needs of table and chairs; dimensions will be at least 8' x 6½'. You can reduce this considerably by using a snack area that takes up only one side.

Peninsula eating area. Allow at least 42" of clearance from its end to the opposite wall, and do not block this passageway with refrigerators or wall ovens or other appliances with doors that open out.

Eating Counter Locations

Consider placing the snack counter along one side of a working peninsula or island, or facing under a window. Be sure the eating area is out of the normal traffic areas for food preparation, or you will defeat your convenience purpose.

You may use an eating counter as a visual separation for a kitchen/dining room combination. Serve small snacks on it, and then have it function as a serving counter for regular meals. One exciting way to integrate such a counter with standard cabinets on the dining area side is to run the dining area carpeting up the cabinet backs to meet the countertop.

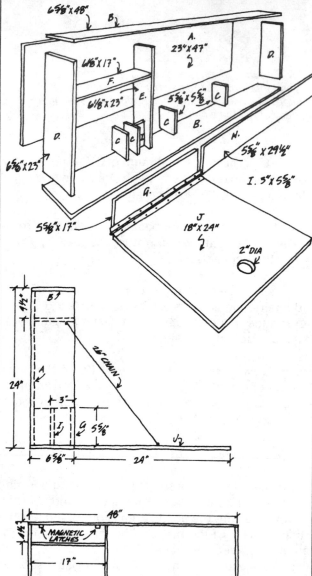

How to Build Your Message Center

1. Cut pieces from the plywood panel according to dimensions.

2. Glue and nail all the smaller partitions into place before assembling larger pieces.

3. To assemble the larger pieces, attach the shelf to brace using the piano hinge and adjust the chain so that the shelf sits level with the chain fully extended.

4. Sand, fill where needed, and paint.

5. Place cup hooks according to what you plan to hang from them, and add cork self-adhesive squares. (Courtesy of Georgia-Pacific)

MESSAGE CENTER

Built-ins offer many customizing options for your kitchen. Some of the projects throughout this book lend themselves to use in this important room, such as the shelf systems and wine racks in the family room section. Wine, however, will not keep as well in a kitchen with warm temperatures as it will in a cooler spot.

Messages can be served up hot or cold, and the kitchen seems to be the logical place for the family message center. Here are the directions for building a handy message center (plans courtesy of Georgia-Pacific). It has a fold-down writing surface and space for a wall-hanging phone.

Tools and materials. One ½'' x 4' x 8' plywood panel A-B or A-C grade; 18'' piano hinge; one link-chain with eye screws (26''); two sets heavy-duty magnetic catches; two cork squares; cup hooks; fine sandpaper; white glue; 6d finishing nails; interior semi-gloss enamel paint.

4
Beautiful Bathrooms

Many of the projects throughout this book can be adapted for bathrooms, as long as the materials used are impervious to moisture. For example, you can turn your bathroom into a mini-gallery by framing inexpensive prints (see framing directions in Chapter Two). Or build in an entire drawer system to create hidden storage for towels (see Chapter One).

The three easy improvements in this chapter are bound to give your bathroom a new look. None call for replumbing or the moving of major fixtures. All will add new zest to a powder room, full bath, or small bath of a master bedroom.

Revamping the bathtub area starts with consideration of the tub or shower. Included in this chapter are suggestions for improving the area surrounding a tub, many of which can be adapted for shower installations. Next, consider your bathroom mirrors. There is no other room in the house that is more easily improved with mirrors. Finally, this chapter includes a simple project for creating additional storage.

An open and airy bathroom with white stucco walls and green plants features colored fixtures. Plants are perfect accessories for bathrooms, because they thrive on airborne moisture. (Courtesy of American Standard Co.)
▼

Ceramic tile covers the walls in this unusual surround/wall/contoured tile bench under a sun lamp. White ceramic mosaics cover contoured bench surface. Tub and lavatories are in French pink. (Photo courtesy of American Olean)

TUB TREATMENTS

In most bathrooms, the tub is the largest element. Your decorative treatment of the tub therefore affects the entire room. Furthermore, any tub surround you install is likely to stay the same for years, while you can change the walls at the drop of a wallcovering or dash of paint. So treatment of the tub area is a key decision in customizing your bathroom.

You will want to choose your tub surround carefully. Your basic choices include high-pressure laminated plastic surrounds and the highly durable and elegant tiles. Both plastic and tiles come in a wealth of colors and patterns—some in new, easier to install systems.

Make sure that your tub surround is set on a firm foundation. Vinyl-surfaced gypsum wallboard, waterproof plaster, or marine plywood are good backings. The surround should be supported so that there is little or no "give," especially when laying up tile. All seams must be carefully sealed with water-resistant adhesives, which also are used for attaching the surround.

Ask about the ease of cleaning your surround material before buying it. This is especially crucial in areas with mineral-rich or extremely hard water. Give careful consideration to any additional features, such as hand holds or soap dishes, that you may wish to install with the surround.

Installing Tile Surrounds

Glazed ceramic tiles are elegant and easily maintained, impervious to constant splashing and washing. You can be creative and design your own patterns with solid tiles, or choose from any number of ready–made design tiles. You can even extend the tiles to encompass parts of the wall and floor. Tile sizes range from 1'' to 1'.

For a simple tile treatment of the bathtub surround, consider the "Redi-Set" systems, which include tiles preset in sheets. These can be ordered specifically for the size of the job, with numbered sheets so that you can put them up in the right sequence. They come in the standard 4¼'' square tiles often used for tubs as well as some other sizes. An appealing feature is that these can be installed directly over existing tiles. Complete instructions come with these tile sheets, as well as the corner strips and additional tiles you will need to complete a handsome job.

Your favorite fixture manufacturer may also provide a surround to go with a new tub. (Photo courtesy of American-Standard)

This plaid pattern uses 4¼" x 4¼" tile, some of which is scored and some plain. (Designed by Rhoda Albom for American Olean)

Before Redi-Set ceramic tile is installed over existing tile, adhesive is spread with a notched trowel over old tile. New grout is highly stain and mildew resistant. (Photo courtesy of American Olean)

Redi-Set pregrouted ceramic tile sheets are easily put into place over gypsum wallboard. Grout joints are prefilled with a flexible silicone rubber grout which will not crack out with building movement. After sheets (about 2' square) are in place, the same grout material is used to finish the installation.

Installing Loose Tiles

Prepackaged, pregrouted sheets may not come in the colors or patterns you want. If so, here are the general directions for installing tiles for a tub surround. You can adapt these directions for installing tiles on a wall or for installing a tile shower stall.

Tools and materials. Tiles, including about one dozen extra, purchased all at the same time to assure matching (identical tiles may vary from batch-to-batch); accessory tiles; one gallon of wall-tile mastic adhesive per 50 square feet; 1 lb. of grout per 18 square feet; notched trowel; straightedge; level; denatured alcohol; cloths; scribing tool; tile nippers or pliers; grout sealer; and masking tape.

Steps

1. Prepare walls, making them as near square as possible. Clean surface of old soap scum, etc., so that mastic will adhere well. Prime with a sealer if necessary. Cover tub with newspaper, etc.

2. Start on the back wall, and find the lowest point of the tub. Mark one tile width above this low point, and extend line from corner to corner. This is your base level line.

3. Plan your tile layout so that full tiles are in the

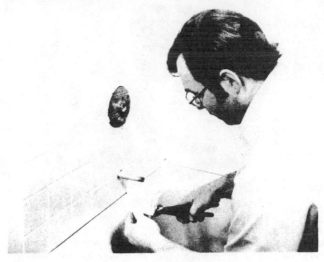

1. Draw a vertical line in middle of back wall and horizontal level line 55½ in. above tub. Also draw a vertical line 32½ in. out from back wall as a guide for spreading adhesive.

4. Use nippers to cut holes for pipe. Clean grout from edges of tiles and replace in sheets.

2. Apply ceramic tile wall adhesive on back wall using notched trowel. Use enough pressure so lines of adhesive are even, and be sure you can intermittently see the lines you drew on the wall.

3. Set sheet No. 1 at lower left corner, minimum of ⅛ in. above tub, within the guidelines drawn. Install remaining sheets 2, 3 and 4 on back wall. Then spread adhesive and apply sheets 5 and 6 on one end wall and sheets 7 and 8 on pipe wall.

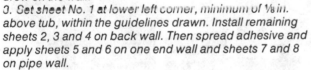

5. Cut tile legs to proper width by scoring along straightedge with glass cutter and nipping along score line with nippers. Outside edges of this tile are glazed so no trim is necessary.

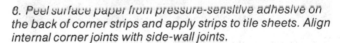

6. Peel surface paper from pressure-sensitive adhesive on the back of corner strips and apply strips to tile sheets. Align internal corner joints with side-wall joints.

7. Grout joints between the sheets, at tub line and corner strips, with grout gun filled with same silicone rubber which was used to pregrout the sheets. Nozzle on gun is made to conform to joint.

8. Caulk with same material around pipe holes.
9. Clean as you go. Joints may be smoothed with finger after spraying with denatured alcohol. Excess silicone rubber on face of tile can be cleaned by going over joint with cheesecloth saturated with alcohol.

10. Completed tub surround looks neat and professional. In this photo, home owner went on to do floor with same material.

11. Here's another example. Redi-Set was used as a wainscot and floor, and fabric was used above for designer effect.

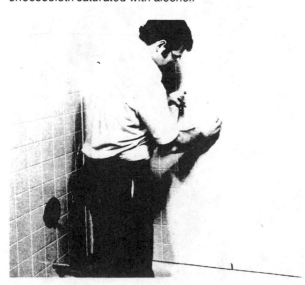

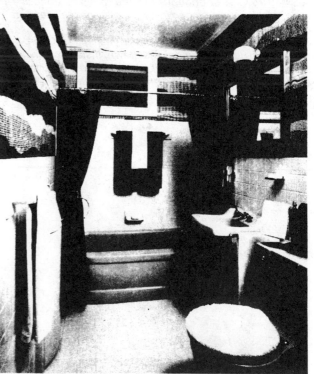

center of the backwall, and any fractions of tiles are equal on both ends. Run vertical lines along both sides of back panel where full tiles will go. Height from top edge of back panel to base level line is usually 56'', to allow for shower spray. Run vertical lines throughout section, marking off smaller (2' to 3') areas to be tiled. Use either masking tape or pencil to mark verticals, using level to create plumb lines. Complete the large grid design with a horizontal line about halfway up the area, or with a number of horizontal lines as guides in placing tiles.

4. Follow similar procedure for end walls, continuing beyond tub and down to floor. Mark perimeter lines, and make a grid to follow within area to be tiled. Tiles extend one row beyond tub ends, or about 32'' from back wall, to accommodate splashing.

5. Start tiling from the bottom up on the back wall. Set one horizontal base line, plus one vertical line along one edge. Spread no more than three square feet of mastic at one time, so that you can tile the area before the mastic sets up.

6. Apply mastic with notched side of the trowel, running full beads across area to be covered. Use a twisting motion of your hand to press the tiles in place and spread mastic behind tile. At the same time be careful not to gouge up mastic so that it gets on the face of the tile. Check each horizontal row with a level before going to the next row.

7. To cut fractional tiles around edges, score with scribing tool on the glazed side and snap them over a straight hard edge, such as a screwdriver or long nail. Check section in Chapter Three on making a tile kitchen counter for further tips on cutting and fitting.

8. Add cap tiles, etc., which are laid up outside the perimeters of the solid tiles. Allow mastic to dry, then finish with grout and sealer as per the directions in Chapter Three on tiling a kitchen counter.

9. Soap dishes, etc., are installed after the tiles.

Create a Platform Tub

A platform tub is one good way of hiding an inelegant or older bathtub, giving a more finished feeling to your bath. You can make it as elaborate as you wish, and cover the platform area to match the decorations used in the rest of the room.

Interior designer Thomas Hills Cook created this platform tub, using bamboo patterned wallcovering plus real bamboo pieces. (Photo courtesy of Armstrong)

Here is a close-up of the platform tub. Recreate it exactly, or use wallcovering to create your own look (Photo courtesy of Armstrong.)

Tools and materials. Molding for base; 2 x 4s to make frame; ½'' marine plywood; nails; waterproof wall-covering; plastic laminate for top; silicone water-proof adhesive; "L" braces if needed.

Steps

1. Decide on overall dimensions of platform wanted. Keep platform height at least ½'' below edge of tub. Measure all along tub for lowest point, and determine platform height from this lowest point.

2. Construct your frame of 2 x 4s, using spacers along edge 16'' to 24'' on center. Nail plywood to 2 x 4s. Secure to walls or floor with "L" braces if unit does not surround tub on all four sides.

3. Make or have made a plastic laminated top, cut out to fit around tub. Extend front edge of top at least 1'' below frame. Use manufacturer's suggested adhesive to adhere top to frame.

4. Cover frame with desired covering.

5. Finish off by sealing between top and tub with silicone sealant, and add molding to base of plat-form.

Variations

- Use redwood or another exterior grade of plywood (which is impervious to water) for the frame of the tub. Or cover with carpeting, such as self-stick squares.
- Complete the look with the addition of an overhead valance with recessed shower curtain rods. Line it up with platform, and decorate to match.

USE MIRRORS EFFECTIVELY

Mirrors for the bathroom can be pretty as well as practical. Consider first the practical angle. You need a mirror over the lavatory, complete with adequate lighting. An additional mirror, installed at another location in the bathroom, can take care of traffic problems. Or you might consider setting up a vanity center in another area altogether, such as in the master bedroom.

Make the most of your mirrors aesthetically, once you have decided where they will work best. Most bathrooms are small scale, and often have proportions that are not basically attractive. Use mirrors to correct visual size and shape. While mirrors enhance large bathrooms, they can work magic in creating a grand scale for powder rooms. Mirror installation methods are discussed in other sections of this book.

This rescued coat closet was doubled visually from its width of 42'' by designer Michael Cannarozzi. The mirrored wall is even more eye-fooling with a half-sun reflected in it, made of Contact-ed plywood. Narrow counter bears a 10'' sink. (Photo courtesy of 1,001 Decorating Ideas)

The mirror tiles over the lavatory are also under, around, and completely covering the lavatory wall. (Photo courtesy of American-Standard) ▶

CREATE GREAT STORAGE

Towels, beauty aids, and electric grooming aids all need their place. Here is a simple wall hanging unit from Georgia-Pacific that can be adapted for use over the toilet, beside the lavatory, or anywhere you need it.

Tools and materials. One sheet ¾" x 4' x 4' Exterior Grade plywood (good two sides); one sheet ¼" x 2' x 4' Exterior Grade plywood (good one side); 1" x 27" wood dowel; two ¼" x 2" wood dowels; one ⅛" x 2' x 3' hardwood panel (door material); ¾" x 8' half-round trim; nails; wood filler; fine sandpaper; stain or interior semi-gloss enamel paint; fasteners for attaching unit to wall.

Steps

1. Cut plywood according to dimensions in illustration.
2. Mark spacing for the shelves on each of the side panels. Then dado each of the side panels, spaced as shown, and drill hole for towel bar.
3. Dado the door grooves in each of the shelves.
4. Sand and paint or stain doors, shelves, and dowels.
5. Assemble the shelves and one side piece, leaving one side off until the doors are placed in the dadoed runners.
6. Attach the remaining side piece and glue and nail into place.
7. Turn structure over, then nail the back panel into the back edges of the shelves, sides, top, and bottom.
8. Attach half-round trim with glue and nails.
9. Sand and paint or stain remaining parts of unit.
10. Attach the optional dowel pegs and towel bar.
11. Attach unit to the wall.

Variations

- Extend the sides of the unit down to floor, up to ceiling, or both.
- Alternate shelves and towel bars on a longer unit.
- Size unit to fit over toilet, extending down both sides.
- Use hardware on doors to match other hardware in bathroom.

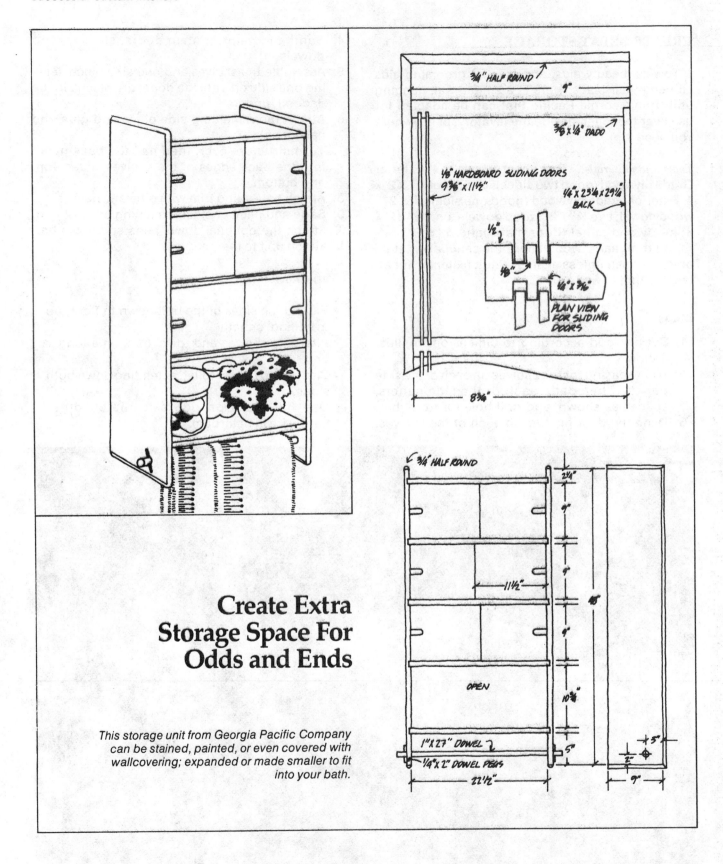

Create Extra Storage Space For Odds and Ends

This storage unit from Georgia Pacific Company can be stained, painted, or even covered with wallcovering; expanded or made smaller to fit into your bath.

5
Bedrooms

A bedroom is your own personal retreat, the one place in the house where you can go for privacy. Here are some projects for making that retreat as attractive as possible, as well as for getting the most out of the space.

The bed is the largest piece of furniture in most bedrooms, making it the decorative focal point. Included here are ways of dressing up the bed with a number of inventive headboard treatments. Most are easy to make, and relatively inexpensive.

Canopy effects can be created without the basic fourposter on which they are traditionally hung. A thorough explanation and plans for making your own ceiling-hung canopy are given.

Platform beds may, at first glance, seem to be mostly for show, but for certain lifestyles and in some bedrooms they solve many problems. You can make a room seem larger by using a sleek-lined furniture unit such as a platform bed. And you may be able to achieve additional storage by elevating the bed and using shelving or drawers underneath. Once the choice mainly of the avante garde, platform beds have become more accepted and increasingly popular.

Finally, included here are the step-by-step means of tailoring and customizing window shades. Make them with sheets or with a decorative fabric of your choice.

DRESSING UP THE BED

Sheet manufacturers have provided great variety in exciting and genuinely pretty designs for the bed. And, they have also shown us how to use these larger fabrics to decorate the entire bedroom.

Since sheets are wider than ordinary fabric, they often cost less per yard than fabrics bought in the "piece goods" department. This means they are easier to use for large projects, such as covering walls, because less seaming is involved.

Coordinating with sheets is easy. Many solids are color-matched to popular prints. Some printed sheets are designed in collections so that they can be mix-matched, combining two or more patterns that are planned for use as a coordinated unit. And, while designer fashions may not be your cup of tea, or may not suit your budget, some of the better known designers have turned their professional attention to sheet designs. You can follow their lead in coordinating your bedroom.

Whatever fabrics you choose to use throughout this room should at least relate to the bedcovering, and perhaps even match it.

In adding a new bed covering, or new sheets, you may discover that something needs to be done to dress up the bed frame itself. Most standard bed frames are fine to use as a base. Customizing then gives the entire unit a new and fresh look. Here are some quick ways of altering headboard or bedstead designs.

Make a Simple Fabric-covered, Padded Headboard

A staple gun and batting, plus the fabric of your choice can convert a plain headboard into a padded version. Use gimp trim if necessary to cover and finish any parts that are raw. Paint the exposed parts, such as posts and foot, to pick up one of the colors of the fabric. You can even make your own headboard from scratch by using ½" plywood panel the width of the bed, supported by legs (such as 1 x 2's) on either side.

Tools and materials. Plywood panel for headboard; support legs; staple gun; polyester quilt batting or polyfoam; fabric for front and back (or muslin for back); gimp if necessary; glue and nails for attaching legs; two-sided tape (optional).

A headboard/room divider, with bookcases built into the back side, creates a study area. Mirror tiles make the small space seem larger. (Photo courtesy of the Armstrong Interior Design Center)

Fabric-covered headboards, curtains, and a spread to match give a totally unified look. You don't even have to start totally from scratch. Montgomery Ward makes the quilted spread, and offers matching fabric for your custom details.

Readymade pillows and a comforter start this scheme, which is completed with a custom headboard, draperies, and tablecloth from matching yard goods. (Photo courtesy of Montgomery Ward Co.) ▶

Steps

1. Cut plywood panel to width of bed, shaped however you wish. Attach legs with glue and nails (or, use your old headboard).

2. Cover headboard with at least two layers of padding, either wrapping padding to the back (about 2'' on top and sides, flush with bottom), or cutting padding to exact size of the headboard. Anchor if needed with two-sided tape.

3. Cut fabric larger than headboard, allowing 3'' extra on top and sides and 1'' below bottom edge. Turn fabric under padding along bottom edge of platform, flush to front. Staple along the bottom, through padding.

4. Pull fabric up and over headboard. Staple in place on back, starting in the center and working to the sides, keeping fabric taut and the grain straight.

5. Miter corners, and staple from center of sides to corners. Finish with gimp if necessary, such as around joining of headboard and legs.

6. Finish back with a matching piece of fabric or muslin by tacking it in place.

7. Attach to bedframe.

Make a Hanging Headboard

This is a solution for studio beds, or even double beds that are flush with the wall.

Tools and materials. ½'' plywood the width of the bed and desired height; 3 layers of batting; fabric; drill; two screws; staple gun.

Steps

1. Cut three layers of batting the size of the board plus 2'' extra on all sides. Cut fabric the size of the board plus 3'' extra on all sides.

2. Find wall studs at head of bed, and drill two holes to accommodate screws. Leave heads of screws sufficiently out from the wall so that board can be suspended from screws, taking into account depth of batting and plywood.

3. Position headboard over bed, mark and measure where screws should meet headboard. Drill holes in headboard for hanging.

4. Place fabric face down on flat surface. Place batting, then board, on fabric. Staple batting in place, then fabric in place, working from centers to corners. Miter corners.

5. Hang on screws through pre-drilled holes.

Truly elegant headboards transform old originals with the addition of fabric plus posts. (Design by Jim deMartin, photo courtesy of 1,001 Decorating Ideas)

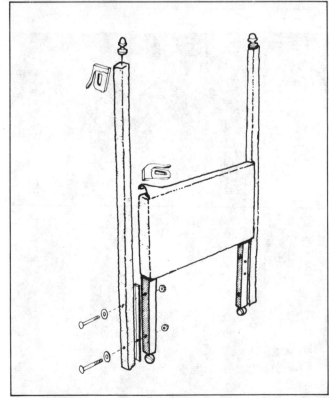

Here is an expanded view of the elements that make up the poster bed headboard. (Courtesy of 1,001 Decorating Ideas)

Make a Fabric-Covered Poster-Bed

Here is a good treatment for either twin or double beds.

Tools and materials. Simple store-bought headboards; 2 x 3's, 6'6'' tall (or shorter if your ceiling height demands it); staple gun; drill; 4 bolts; drapery rod ends.

Steps

1. Wrap headboard with fabric, stapling in back.

2. Wrap fabric around 2 x 3 posts, stapling snugly down the back of the 3'' side of the 2 x 3.

3. Drill holes through posts and bolt to headboard legs.

4. Add drapery finials to post tops.

5. Bolt headboard to frame.

82

Who says headboards have to be conventional in size? This modern design will give dreams of pyramid power. (Photo courtesy of Simmons Company)

Go Modern with a Pyramid Headboard

This headboard is both Egyptian and contemporary in feeling. It is a good solution for platform beds, which often do not come with headboards.

Tools and materials. Solid-color sheeting; lathing strips to support plywood; ½" plywood cut in a huge triangular shape; ½" x 1" strips to edge two top edges; staples; two-sided tape; small nails; picture hanger.

Steps

1. Cut plywood into triangular shape, using lathing strips to join pieces, making triangle large enough by nailing and gluing the strips to the back.

2. Cover entire triangle with solid sheeting, wrapping to back and stapling, with a 2" margin at the back.

3. Cut strips of matching fabric to cover edging strips 4" wider, and 3" longer, than edging strips. Run two-sided tape along 1" face of edging strip, on both sides of strip. Press fabric along one side, fabric edge adhering to edge of strip.

4. Nail edging strip into edge of plywood so that fabric on edging falls towards front of headboard. Allow edging strip to protrude beyond headboard ½" x ½". Carefully wrap edging fabric over edging, pressing into place along outside surface on two-sided tape. Wrap edging fabric to the back and staple to plywood headboard panel.

5. Attach picture hangers near top of finished headboard and anchor to wall (since triangle rests on the floor, further anchoring is not needed).

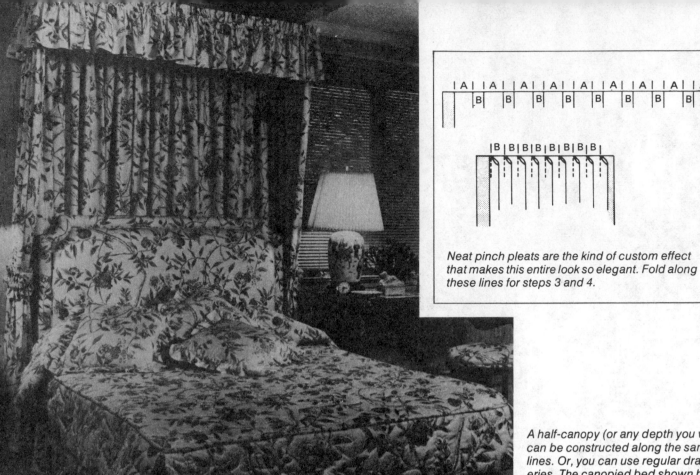

| A | A | A | A | A | A | A | A | A |

| B | B | B | B | B | B | B | B |

| B | B | B | B | B | B | B | B |

Neat pinch pleats are the kind of custom effect that makes this entire look so elegant. Fold along these lines for steps 3 and 4.

A half-canopy (or any depth you wish) can be constructed along the same lines. Or, you can use regular draperies. The canopied bed shown here is covered with fabric to match and soften the elegant Pecky Cypress White hardboard paneling with biege over white graining. (Photo courtesy of Masonite Corp.)

This canopy bed doubles for storage, with hidden space over the bed. 4 x 4's make the frame, which is attached to the ceiling with molding. The luxurious carpeting is simple to install 12'' carpet squares. (Designed by Louise Cowan, courtesy of the Armstrong Interior Design Center)

This elegant canopy extends to the four corners of the bed in sheets to match. (Photo courtesy of Springmaid)

CANOPY EFFECTS

If you do not have a fourposter, you can create a canopy effect by using the walls and ceiling. This idea will work equally well in a modern or traditional room, depending on your choice of fabric.

A Simple Canopy Effect

A simple canopy can be made by attaching two rods to the ceiling (one next to the wall where the bed is to be placed, and the other farther out into the room over the bed). Hooks and dowels are suitable for rods (or conventional curtain rods). Run fabric the width of the bed, up over the rod at ceiling/wall joint, then stretch it or drape it in a graceful curve to the next rod. Allow sufficient fabric to hang down over the front of the second rod (about a foot or more, depending upon your ceiling height).

Fabric should be attractive on both sides, since the reverse will show on the front edge. Use doubled fabric, or a fabric such as felt that looks well on either side.

Finish the front edge with some detailing that adds to the overall style. Curves, points with tassles, or contrasting trim are easy suggestions.

If fabric is extended far into the room across the ceiling, you may want to anchor it to the front rod with two-sided tape, staples or tacks. The weight of the fabric going down the wall should keep it anchored on the back. Tack fabric at baseboard level for extra security.

Create a Bed Canopy and Draperies

A "total" bed canopy attached to the ceiling with draperies at each corner, creates an exciting and private haven for the bed. You can alter the design to suit your own needs (for example, make a demi-canopy by using draperies only on the two sides of the headboard). Here are the plans for making the full canopy and draperies as they appear, from Springs Mills. The fabric used is, of course, Springmaid Sheets.

Tools and materials. One double and two queen-size Springmaid "Shadows" flat sheets; one queen-size and three king-size Springmaid Wondercale white flat sheets; 68 snap fasteners with attaching tool; 7½ yards 1" wide twill tape; 18½ yards Conso "Shirrite" tape; six 18" sash rods with brackets and screws; drapery hooks to fit over rods; 1" x 4" pine in two pieces 54" and two 74"; 1" x 1" pine in four pieces 54" and four 74"; ¼" x 1¾" lattice strips in four pieces 54" and four 74"; 1" x 1¼" finishing nails; 16 toggle bolts; staple gun; paint to match ceiling.

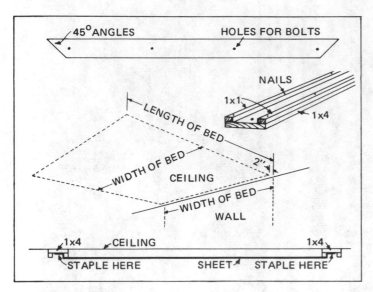

To create the canopy, use 1 x 4's as illustrated for step 1 through 4 below.

Steps for Canopy

1. Cut a 45 degree angle at both ends of each 1 x 4; bore four holes, evenly spaced along center of each, for toggle bolts. With 1¼" nails, attach a 1 x 1 flush with outside edge along both sides of each 1 x 4; cut ends of 1 x 1 flush with 1 x 4 and paint all surfaces.

2. On ceiling, mark outline to same size as bed for placement of sides and front of frame; mark a line to indicate a 2" space between the point where the wall and ceiling meet at the head of the bed and the beginning of the canopy frame (this is to allow space for the fabric).

3. Cut a 55" length of twill tape; turn ends under 1" and attach half a snap fastener ½" from each end, then every 4" along center of tape. Staple tape along one 54" part of frame with top edge of tape along top of 1 x 4. Using toggle bolts, attach this part to ceiling so back edge with tape is 2" out from wall; attach other three parts of frame to ceiling so all corners meet. Using double "Shadows" sheets, staple one edge in space between two 1 x 1's on side of frame; stretch sheet across frame; staple to frame on other side, and across top and bottom, so it is stretched taut; cut away excess fabric.

4. Attach half a snap fastener to center of remaining twill tape every 4"; staple tape to frame around three sides with top edge against ceiling. Paint

lattice strips; nail between two 1 x 1's to cover edge of sheet.

5. Attach one sash rod on either side of frame at head end, and two at each corner, using screws through lattice into 1 x 4.

6. Cut eight 13" wide crosswise strips from the queen-size sheet for ruffle. Seam two strips together along 13" edge for back of canopy. Seam other six strips together for outside ruffle. Attach snaps to shirring tape. Turn side hems and attach shirring tape to ruffle. At one end of ruffle, turn ½" to wrong side, then turn 1" hem; stitch. Turn 1" to wrong side along top edge of strip; pin top edge of tape along fold so first snap is ½" from end. Continue to other end. Stitch along each side of tape.

7. Cut each of the "Shadows" sheets into nine 9" wide lengthwise strips for border; matching design, seam nine strips together as shown; trim ½" outside of seam; press. Turn ½" to wrong side along each edge; fold in half lengthwise so inside is slightly wider; press.
   Pin border along bottom so edge of ruffle is along center fold of border; turn raw ends in; stitch close to fold along top edge.

8. Drive a nail into wall at each side of bed behind ruffle; pull up strings of shirring tape; snap ruffle to frame; wrap strings back and forth over nails to hide them behind canopy so ruffle may be opened flat later for washing.

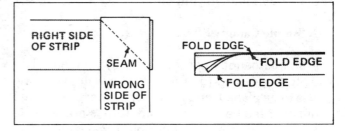

Attach strips for step 8, above, to make a continuous length of fabric to make ruffles. Then fold as illustrated.

Steps for Draperies

1. Cut selvages off remaining sheets; cut two to 103" wide and cut one into two 49½" widths. On each narrow width, turn ½" to wrong side, then turn a 1" hem along one edge. Seam remaining border strips together and make border as for canopy.

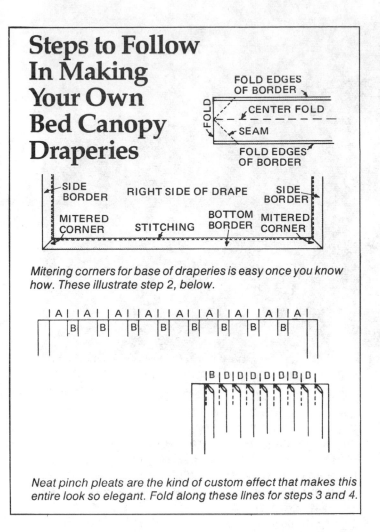

Steps to Follow In Making Your Own Bed Canopy Draperies

FOLD EDGES OF BORDER
FOLD
CENTER FOLD
SEAM
FOLD EDGES OF BORDER

SIDE BORDER — RIGHT SIDE OF DRAPE — SIDE BORDER
MITERED CORNER — STITCHING — BOTTOM BORDER — MITERED CORNER

Mitering corners for base of draperies is easy once you know how. These illustrate step 2, below.

| A | | A | | A | | A | | A | | A | | A | | A | | A |

| B | | B | | B | | B | | B | | B | | B | | B |

| B | | D | D | D | D | D | D | D | D |

Neat pinch pleats are the kind of custom effect that makes this entire look so elegant. Fold along these lines for steps 3 and 4.

2. Place border down one side of a full width and mark bottom corner; miter border by folding border wrong side out at mark; stitch at 45 degree angles from center fold to each edge; trim ½" outside of seam.

   Measure 103" from first miter and form second corner; press seams. Place border around three sides with edge of drape along center fold of border; stitch close to fold edge of border.

3. Hold drape up to rod on canopy and determine proper finished length. Turn a double 6" hem across top, cutting away excess fabric. Mark pinch pleats across top edge, using 7" for A and 4" for B, as per illustration. Fold A sections in half, bringing B lines together; stitch 6" down from top edge. Fold fullness of each pleat into three equal smaller folds; stitch across lower edge of folds; catch-stitch inside of fold at top.

4. On each half width, attach border along bottom and raw side edge, then pleat top edge so there

are four pleats with 4" each end. Pin drapery hooks to each pleat and both side edges; hang drapery hooks over rods.

Variations

- Use ready-made draperies instead of sheets. Make sure you choose draperies that are equally attractive inside and out.
- Make a demi-canopy using just side and back draperies, and extending canopy only about 1½' away from the wall.
- Use a neutral solid-colored fabric for the panel across the ceiling, and make more than one set of canopy ruffles and draperies. Since they snap off and flatten for storage and cleaning, you can vary sheets for summer and winter or alternate sets all year long.

PLATFORM BEDS

Modern and informal are the two adjectives that best describe platform beds. Covered with carpeting, they make a lounging area for daytime that is as functional as possible, and provide healthy sleeping at night. Carpeting also offers easy maintenance and quiet acoustics.

Low, Wide-Box Platform With Backrest

Use same-color carpeting for bed platform, or contrasting color in the same grade, to set it off. Alter the size to suit your room's dimensions.

Tools and materials. ½" plywood; two 4' x 8' sheets for top, one 6" x 8' panel for top of headrest, two 30" x 8' for back and front of headrest; ¾" plywood in two 8' x 11" planks; two 7'10½" x 11" planks; five 2 x 6's 26" long; nine 2 x 6's 7'10½" long; two 2 x 6's 8' long; staple gun; carpet tape; nails and glue.

Steps

1. Assemble headrest first. Use 8' 2 x 6's for top and bottom frame, with 26" 2 x 6's spaced between them and on ends. Attach ½" plywood to front, back, and top with nails and glue, nailing into spacers as well as frame.

2. Nail and glue side 2 x 6's (7'10½" long) to equally long side plywood. Place 2 x 6 supports on top of base side 2 x 6's, and nail 8' x 11" plywood head and foot to sides. Space 2 x 6 supports so that seam between two top ½" plywood sheets is over

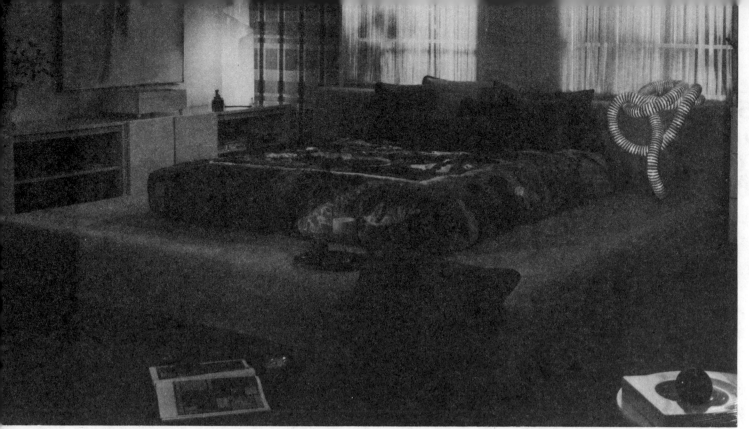

A carpeted platform with a simply covered mattress makes a bedroom a wonderful lounge area as well. (Photo courtesy of Allied Chemical)

one support, remainder evenly distributed. Nail and glue supports to side panels.

3. Nail and glue top ½" plywood sheets over frame.

4. Attach headrest to platform with nails and glue.

5. Attach carpeting with carpet adhesive tape or staples along floor lines, etc. Miter corners for platform front and use carpet adhesive tape to create invisible seams. Use same technique to cover headrest.

CREATING EXTRA STORAGE

Is there ever a bedroom that has enough storage? Especially these days, when bedrooms serve more than one purpose and also function as studys, sewing rooms, home offices, or even miniature laundry rooms. Here are some ideas for increasing your bedroom storage areas. These storage areas are constructed of Louisiana Pacific redwood plowed fascia (if you buy it already plowed you can cut down considerably on construction time). And, if you use it creatively, it will add greatly to the decorative impact of your room.

Notes on Working with Redwood Plowed Fascia

The fascia is available in nominal ¾" or 2" thicknesses, and 6" or 8" in width. It is made of short lengths of clean lumber end-glued into long pieces with interesting natural grain and color variations. Finger joints where lengths are joined and glued make an extremely strong joint. The material comes in either single or double plow patterns with $5/16$" or $7/16$" wide grooves, set ⅝" from the outside edge.

Cut with either a sharp, fine-toothed hand or power saw blade. Use either small-headed finish or large-headed common nails. Pre-drill holes to avoid splitting for screws, and use wood screws. Use standard wood glue in addition to nails or screws. Sand lightly with fine grade paper to remove sharp edges and fingerprints.

Finish by using clear finishes such as lacquer, varnish, polyurethane or wax; or any stained finish that is penetrating, wiping on wax. Paint finishes should be latex-based or oil-based. You can leave it unfinished, but a protective coat will avoid stains.

Under-Bed Storage

Make a simple box on casters and slide it under the bed for hidden storage. You may want to make these for beds throughout the house.

Tools and materials. ¾" fascia with $7/16$" groove, width determined by clearance under the bed; ½" plywood for box bottom; four ½" plywood blocks to brace corners and support casters; flatheaded nails;

Another variation on the platform theme raises the bed area so that storage can be tucked underneath. The platform frames furniture, with dead storage behind it. (Courtesy Allied Chemical)

Simple underbed storage can be as fancy or as no-fuss as you wish. This storage box slips out easily on wheels. (Design by Louisiana-Pacific Corp.)

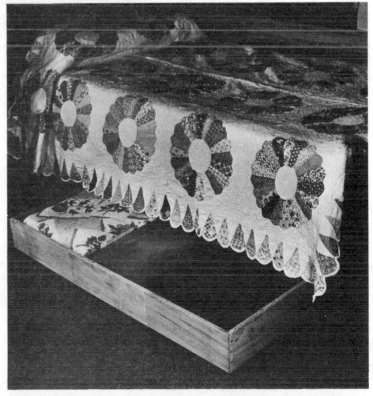

glue; four casters; fine sandpaper; finish of your choice.

Steps

1. Cut two long sides and two end pieces of fascia, miter corners.

2. Sand edges of plywood so that it will fit into fascia groove.

3. Assemble box by nailing and gluing fascia together at corners (or use screws).

4. Attach blocks in corners with nails and glue, sized large enough to accommodate casters.

5. Attach casters as suggested by caster manufacturer.

6. If you plan to keep heavy items in the box, add a fifth caster in the bottom center.

7. Finish with clear finish.

Variations

• Cover the box in fabric, to match your bed-

89

These are the simple components for making a drawer with pre-plowed redwood fascia. (Photo courtesy of Louisiana-Pacific Corp.)

You can use the fascia with double plowed grooves, add your own decorative molding to the grooves, and achieve a truly custom effect. (Photo courtesy of Louisiana-Pacific Corp.)

room. Add a dust cover of the same fabric to go over the top. Make dust cover with 1'' hems, sized to overlap front and back of box 1''. Staple fabric along back edge of box, bring over box, and add snaps along front edge.

• Decorate box with Early American stencils or decals.

• Add decorative molding to box, painted in a contrasting color to box sides.

Make storage drawers for wherever you need them

Here are the basics for making drawers with fascia. They are sturdy, but require no expensive power tools or craftsperson's skill to create. With fascia, a simple box with ¼'' or ⅜'' on the bottom becomes a drawer.

Tools and materials. Plywood for drawer floor; fascia for four sides; drawer pull; nails and glue; finish.

Steps

1. Decide first how you want to make the joints at drawer corners. Here are the alternatives, which are most important for the drawer front where seam will show:

   A. Make a butt joint nailed and glued from the side, but the end grain of the sides will show at front.

   B. Make a butt joint fastened and glued from the front. Fill and sand nail or screw holes.

   C. Rabbet the sides into the drawer front to conceal end grains.

   D. Dado the sides into the drawer front.

   E. Use 45 degree mitered angle corners on drawer front.

   F. Add an additional piece of wood to add to box to be the front.

2. Using whichever technique best suits your purpose, make the drawer.

3. Finish with a finish and drawer pull.

Suspended drawers

To suspend a drawer beneath a table, desk, or bench top, screw a small hardwood strip on the top outside edge of the drawer sides. A support track can be made with an "L" shaped wood strip, or a metal "Z" strip attached to the top. Remember to wax sliding parts for smooth operation.

Stacked drawers

A simple box of ¾'' plywood is all that is needed for desk and storage units. Make it with inside dimensions that match those of the number of drawers you have in mind. Assemble fascia drawers with grooves on the outside and screw the bottom of drawer into place. Attach "L" shaped metal angles screwed on the box side for drawers to ride on, and wax sliding parts.

Storage Find: Refinish Furniture

Dress up discarded furniture "finds" with a new coat of paint to match your bedroom and add decorative trim that is in keeping with your decor. You will enhance the room as well as create additional storage space for yourself.

Tools and materials. Fine sandpaper; plastic wood; semi-gloss or gloss enamel; wood glue; small brads. If the paint on the piece is in poor condition, remove it with a paste-type remover and a putty knife or scraper, and sand before applying an undercoat.

Steps

1. Remove paint or old finish if necessary, as suggested above.

2. If paint has only minor scratches or gouges, fill by using plastic wood and sand smooth before applying undercoat.

3. Allow undercoat to dry, sand lightly, and apply coat.

4. Cut molding to size desired and paint, allow to dry.

5. Attach molding with wood glue and small brads. Countersink brads $1/16$", fill each indentation with wood putty, allow to dry, and retouch.

WINDOW TREATMENTS

Window treatments in the bedroom are important decorative accents, but are also crucial for proper sleep. You will want to be able to adjust the amount of light and the amount of ventilation that comes through your window treatment. What follows here is one suggestion for fabric-decorated shades. But, be daring and consider everything including shutters, blinds, and curtains. Or even leave the windows bare and fill them with a variety of hanging plants.

Fabric-cover your shades

You will find shades specifically designed and prepared for the application of fabric in department stores and specialty shade shops. Sheets are ideal for lamination, as well as fabrics that are closely woven (not too sheer, or too thick).

The following directions are from Joanna Western Mills Company for creating a Lam-Eze Laminated shade.

Keep in mind that all-over fabric patterns are easier to work with than stripes or plaids because of the

Contrasting "rope-style" molding wood is painted white for trim. That, plus new hardware, revamped the old dresser. (Photo courtesy Klise)

precision that straight lines demand. If the plan is for 2 or more patterned fabric shades in the same room, allow 18 inches (a standard repeat size) of extra length per shade, so that the pattern design will appear in a uniform position throughout. When only one shade is involved, allow ¼ yard of extra length to allow for trimming top and bottom edges straight across fabric.

All fabrics should be 2 to 4 inches wider than the cloth width of the finished shade. Fabrics most suited for lamination are thin, smooth, closely woven textures with "body".

Tools and materials. Sharp, medium size shears; yard stick; pencil; scotch or drafting tape; cold iron and/or rolling pin; several small heavy objects; saw; true right angle (the cardboard back off any notebook or writing tablet will do); clean flat area for laminating process; wood or steel rule for measuring.

Fabric covered shades in this bedroom are the best balance for the heavy, massive furniture. (Photo courtesy of Lam-Eze Window Shades)

Fabric covered shades also are handsome methods for softening large windows, when combined with draperies. (Photo courtesy of Allied Chemical)

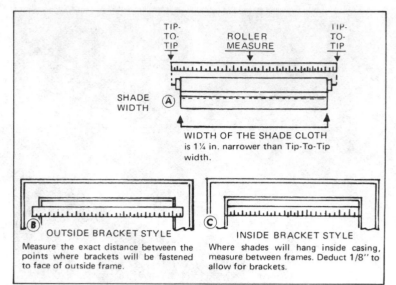

TIP-TO-TIP — ROLLER MEASURE — TIP-TO-TIP

SHADE WIDTH (A)

WIDTH OF THE SHADE CLOTH is 1¼ in. narrower than Tip-To-Tip width.

(B) OUTSIDE BRACKET STYLE
Measure the exact distance between the points where brackets will be fastened to face of outside frame.

(C) INSIDE BRACKET STYLE
Where shades will hang inside casing, measure between frames. Deduct 1/8" to allow for brackets.

Measuring is the most important step in making sure any shade fits and hangs properly. Make sure your measurements of the shade and bracket position are accurate.

Steps—Measuring

1. To determine exact shade size, it is best to install brackets first, then to cut roller to size. If the shade is to hang between window jambs, hang brackets with open end of the slot bracket on left side as you face the window. Fasten the brackets at least 1½" from the top of the window to allow the shade ample room to roll up without binding at the top. Hang the pin end (bracket with round hole) at right side of window in the same manner.

2. If shade is to be hung from face of trim (outside measure), hang projection-type brackets with at least 1½" overlap on each side to provide for adequate coverage of the window when shade is drawn. The open end (slot) bracket is to the left when facing window; pin end bracket to the right.

3. Now measure distance between the two brackets, using a steel tape measure. Make sure there is no sag in the tape. Unroll shade until roller is exposed and detach enough shade cloth from roller to allow for sawing. Cut the roller to this length. Slip cap over roller, insert pin and tap it home with hammer. Check size by placing roller in brackets to insure proper fit. Trim away shade cloth to fit roller, removing a strip to the full length of the cloth equal to the width sawed off the wood roller end. Cloth will then match shortened roller.

4. Length should be 12" longer than desired lower edge position when shade is fully drawn. Should you need to shorten the shade, cut off fabric from the top edge (where attached to roller), so you keep the lower edge of the shade cloth perfectly squared, and untouched.

Steps for Attaching Fabric

1. Use a dry iron to pre-press any creases, wrinkles, or fold marks from the decorative fabric. Spread decorator fabric to be laminated face down on table top. Then in pencil, draw a line lengthwise down the center of fabric from top to bottom. (Skip this step where fabric is too transparent).

2. Check bottom edge of the fabric intended for shade hem with corner square (cardboard) to be sure it is cut perfectly even and straight across material. Then, notch out a small "V-cut" in the exact center of this edge.

3. Roll the decorator fabric onto a cardboard tube, face side in, from top to bottom.

4. Unroll Lam-Eze Shade, face side up on table top, and lightly mark off in pencil (on the surface of the clear plastic "skin") the exact center of the shade cloth from roller to hemline. Re-roll shade and place it on table top, leaving about 18 inches of the shade fabric exposed at the bottom or hem edge, marked side up.

5. Anchor outer corners to table with tape or weights. Lay plastic hem strip across shade just

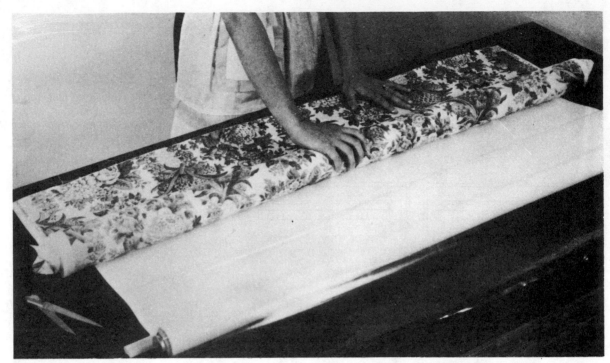

Peel back and trim away a section of clear plastic, exposing the gummed surface (Step 7).

Carefully return decorator fabric to position over gummed surface and smooth with palms of hands to adhere (Step 8).

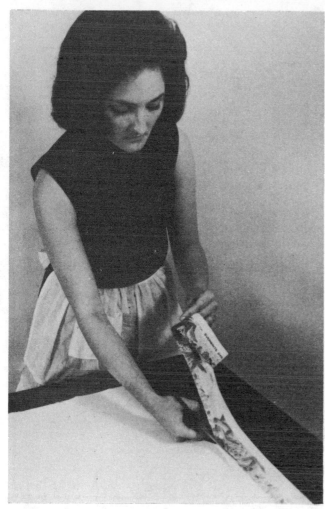

Reverse shade and trim away additional fabric at sides (Step 11).

Finish lower hem by using two-part plastic trim hem (Step 12).

below rolled portion to control tendency of shade to roll up during operations.

6. Lay tube with decorator fabric across the exposed section of the shade. Unroll about 12 inches and line up bottom edges of decorator fabric and Lam-Eze, with the "V-cut" of fabric at the center line of Lam-Eze. Weight down fabric to hold in position for the next step.

7. Carefully fold back about 6 inches of decorator fabric to expose underlying shade cloth. Starting at an outer corner of shade, loosen, and peel back and trim away about a 3-inch deep section of the clear plastic "skin" to expose the gummed surface.

8. Return decorator fabric into position over this exposed 3-inch wide gummed area to anchor it in place. Smooth down decorator fabric with palms of hands, using an upward and outward movement from shade center to sides. EXERCISE CARE AND PRECISION HERE.

9. Resting roll of decorator fabric out of harm's way on the already laminated portion of the shade, peel back an additional 12-inch section of clear plastic. Lay the peeled plastic back over the roller, out of the way. Now, carefully unroll the decorator fabric onto the newly exposed gummed surface, lining up the marked-off center of the fabric with that of the shade.

10. Smooth and press fabric onto shades on newly laminated section. Should unwanted air bubbles form, carefully peel back the fabric, then reapply and smooth. Avoid stretching or distorting the fabric when peeling it back. Complete and repeat the process until entire length of shade has been covered with decorator fabric, taking 12-inch sections one at a time. Go over each newly laminated area with a cold iron, pressing fabric to fabric and smooth out any air pockets, as you work along.

11. Reverse the completely laminated shade on the table top, face down, and carefully trim away the excess decorator fabric extending down both sides of the shade.

12. Finish lower hem by using two-part plastic hem. Insert the corner of bottom edge of shade into open end of U-shaped plastic hem Unit A, and slide it all the way across the shade bottom. Trim away excess of strip. Fold Unit A over once, then insert fold and strip into open end of plastic hem strip Unit B, slide it all the way across shade bot-

tom, and trim away excess overhang with a hacksaw. Lower edge of shade is completed.

13. If you have shortened shade, reattach to roller with staples, tacks, or 2-way tape.

14. To install, roll up shade by hand and place in brackets. Pull shade part-way down to check tension. If shade doesn't roll up with enough tension, pull it half-way down, and remove brackets in this position, then roll up by hand and replace in brackets. If shade has too much tension, remove from brackets in a rolled-up position, then unroll by hand to 50% extended position, replace in brackets, and check. Repeat again if necessary.

Variations

• Instead of using the conventional roll, consider a reverse roll. Shade heading is behind the shade in this type of installation. Be sure to specify that you want reverse roll brackets, which are constructed differently than conventional ones.

• Use a series of shades separated with lambrequins or draperies to unify several windows, or to personalize a large window, or to hide storage.

Create this open door with paint. (Designed by Michael Cannarozzi, courtesy of 1001 Decorating Ideas Magazine)

This tiny powder room is a mere 42" wide, but width is doubled with the use of mirrors. (Courtesy of Michael Cannarozzi Decorating Ideas Magazine)

Colorful molding and a wainscot treatment make this bathroom delightfully Early American in feeling. (Courtesy of American-Standard)

You can cheat a bit, and use readymade spreads plus yard goods to create your own custom effect. (Spread and fabric for the headboard, etc., courtesy of Montgomery Ward Co.)

Two types of scrubbable vinyl laminate wallcovering are used to lower the celing visually in this dining area. The wallcoverings are from the "Small Wonders" collection courtesy of James Seeman Studios, Inc.

Fabric covered shades are the ideal decorating solution for this bedroom which features the newer, massive furniture. (Furniture is Sugar Hill's ready to assemble Dartmouth Collection. Lam-Eze window Shades by Joanna)

Fixtures in a soft beige are emphasized in the contemporary bathroom through the use of mirror tiles. Note especially the handsome double reflection of the sleek sink. (Courtesy American-Standard)

Truly elegant headboards transform old headboards, and can be created with the addition of fabric plus posts. (Designed by Jim DeMartin courtesy of 1001 Decorating Ideas Magazine)

This "L" shaped banquette corner increases in visual size when mirror tiles are installed on the wall above.
(Photo courtesy of Goodyear Floortiles)

Paneling planned in diagonal as well as conventional treatments creates exciting accent walls. This paneled effect employs woodstrips. (Courtesy of Pope and Talbot, Inc.)

Contemporary furnishings are set on the diagonal and backed with carpet-covered cubes and triangles for this innovative and spacious living room arrangement. (Courtesy of Ethan Allen Co.)

A half canopy can be constructed using regular draperies and ruffles. This elegant treatment is the ideal counterpoint to the white hardboard paneling. (Courtesy of Masonite Corp.)

Natural Belgian linen wallcovering creates an interesting textural effect and is a subtle background for earth-toned furnishings. (Photo courtesy of the Belgian Linen Association)

6
Eating Areas & Dining Rooms

Fast food eating may be fine when you are on the run, but has no place at home—at least not for main meals. Psychologically and physically, it is important that you have an attractive place to enjoy family meals and entertain guests.

Spacious dining rooms with attendant legions of help are relics of the past for most of us. The projects in this chapter are designed to let your dining area meet today's needs.

Here are plans for expanding your dining room space through banquettes and visual illusions. A relatively simple divider will allow you to make a dining room multipurpose (perhaps with a music or reading area on the other side of the divider). The same divider will give a sense of privacy to your dining area if it is part of the kitchen or part of an open living room plan.

Attractive lighting is such a key factor in presenting food in an appetizing manner that special attention is given to it. Dimmers are discussed, along with suggestions for lighting treasured objects while providing additional lighting for the room itself. And a ceiling dome that looks centuries old may be just the element to make your ordinary dining room special.

For convenience, dining accessories should be stored in the dining room, a practice that cuts down on the clutter in kitchen cabinets. This chapter gives plans for an entire storage wall.

A roll-around caddy for serving is the kind of article most people wish they had, and once they have one, they wonder how they ever served meals without it. The caddy described here is extra ample, with handles on either end.

EXPAND YOUR DINING ROOM SPACE

Visual effects and built-ins are good ways to make the most of small dining space. The following projects will expand your dining area.

Make Built-in Banquettes

Banquettes, or built-in benches along a wall, allow you to move a table to the side of the room. Use a banquette along one wall, in a popular "L" shape on two walls, or even in a three-sided "U".

Tools and materials. Nails; ¾" plywood; 2 x 4s for framing; sandpaper; glue; wood filler; foam slabs for back and seats (or pillows); fabric; fabric glue.

Steps

1. Cut and make a frame of 2 x 4s for banquette. Make length as long as space to be filled, and height to match height of your dining chairs, minus height of foam slabs. (Note: adjust height to take into consideration that you may sink into banquette seats more than free chairs; plan height to be identical when both seats are used, not when foam slab is empty.)

2. Cut ¾" plywood to fit around front and sides of frame. Attach by nailing and gluing joints. Sand and fill raw ends with filler.

3. The simplest method for creating seating is to nail a plywood board across the top. To create storage beneath banquette, cut side and front panels ¾" higher than frame. Top panel will then fit inside sides. Drill finger holes for removing top panel when necessary. For a long banquette, use several top panels that can be easily removed.

4. Cover entire frame with fabric. Cover matching pillows or foam slabs with fabric. Use matching fabric to cover dining chairs to be used with the banquette, and a coordinating fabric for tablecloths or placemats.

In this eat-in photo gallery, carpeting covers the banquette for a modern look. Pillows pick up the background colors of the photos. (Room designed by Richard W. Jones, FASID, for Eastman Kodak Co.)

Variations

- Use puffy pillows for the banquette instead of foam slabs for a more casual and opulent look.
- Cover the base with carpet to match dining area carpet.
- Use webbing instead of a plywood panel for more comfortable seating on the banquette. To install webbing, lap or dowel corner joints of top of frame, and make it flush with front and side panels. Attach webbing with carpet tacks. Run the webbing from back to front and from side to side, interweaving in both directions, and spacing about 1'' apart. Either canvas or rubber webbing can be used with ⅝'' carpet tacks.

Visual Effects

Many dining areas are rooms or alcoves with small dimensions, awkward to view even when adjoining another larger area such as the living room or the kitchen. To create a more graceful relationship between the walls and ceiling, use visual magic. Here are some good techniques.

Use mirrors to double the apparent size of the dining area.

Create a strong horizontal visual line by seemingly

106

dropping the ceiling. One method is to run molding around the ceiling below the ceiling wall joint, and then to paint the top part of the wall the same color as the ceiling. Another is to use wallpaper creatively, to create a horizontal line at the upper wall line.

Use chair rails to draw the eye to the lower part of the wall. Chair rails are ideal for homes with a bit of heritage in their decor. Chair rail molding is installed at the height of the top of a chair back to protect the wall from being scraped, so serves an additional practical purpose. Add to the horizontal line of a chair rail by using a contrasting color or pattern below the rail to the one above it.

USING ROOM DIVIDERS

This simple divider, with cabinet underneath, can be made in multiples to cover however much space is needed to set off the dining area. The open top serves as a pass-through. Use the cabinet facing the dining area to store linens, etc. Or alternate dividers and have some cabinets facing into the dining area, others into the kitchen or another room. Diagonal treatment on cabinet doors makes this unit elegant.

Construction

Overall width of the divider is 36'', depth is 16'', and height is 6½', or whatever height is best for your home (plans from Georgia-Pacific).

Tools and materials   One panel (good two sides) ¾'' x 4' x 8' Interior grade plywood; one panel ⅝'' x 4' x 8' texture 1-11 plywood; one piece 1'' x 1'' x 6' lumber; one piece 1'' x 1'' x 8' lumber; one ¼'' x 6' dowel; four pairs pin cabinet hinges; four cabinet pulls; four cabinet catches; white glue; nails; magnetic catch plates.

Steps

1. Cut texture 1-11 plywood for diagonal application. Cut panel in half crosswise, then cut the two squares in half diagonally. Cut doors from these. Cut four doors 17³/₁₆'' wide by 24'' high.

2. To make frame, draw parts on Interior grade plywood. Use a compass (or string, tack, and pencil) to trace a pattern for identical corner curves. When cutting, place the panel face up for a hand or table saw, face down for a portable power saw.

3. Cut shelves, noting that the top and bottom of the storage cabinet compartments are wider than the

Banquettes can be short or long, straight or "L" shaped, and are little more difficult to make than building a box. This banquette corner benefits from fabric covering on the banquettes as well as cushions. Floor tiles, self-stick white, cover the floor and banquette bases. (Design by Lois Munroe Hoyt, FASID; Photo courtesy of Goodyear floor tiles)

shelf inside. The extra width is the thickness of the doors, which are ⅝''. Top, bottom, and high shelf are 12'' wide, middle shelf is 10¾''. Notch corners of the middle shelf to accommodate hinge strips.

4. Glue and nail the vertical 1 x 1 hinge strips to divider sides. Fasten shelves in place with ¼'' dowels glued in place. Start by drilling holes in side panels first, then use these holes as a guide to drill into shelf edges.

5. Hang doors, using hidden pivot-type cabinet door hinges from your local lumber dealer. First attach hinges to hinge strip. Place door alongside hinges in an open position. Insert screwdriver tip under door to provide closure clearance, then mark hinge legs position on the door. Saw slots in the door to desired depth to conceal the hinge legs.

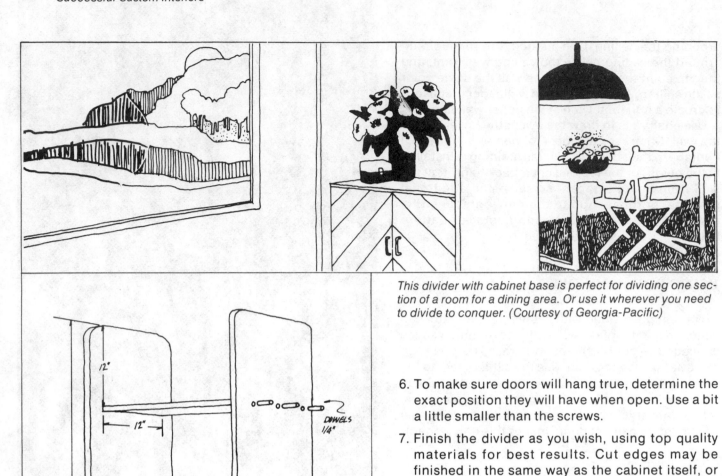

This divider with cabinet base is perfect for dividing one section of a room for a dining area. Or use it wherever you need to divide to conquer. (Courtesy of Georgia-Pacific)

6. To make sure doors will hang true, determine the exact position they will have when open. Use a bit a little smaller than the screws.

7. Finish the divider as you wish, using top quality materials for best results. Cut edges may be finished in the same way as the cabinet itself, or covered with adhesive-backed plastic laminate or wood veneer strips.

8. Add door handles and magnetic catch plates.

Variations

- Install shades to totally block pass-through area on some units.
- Hang plants from the top shelf; add a plant light beneath shelf.
- Wallpaper cabinet fronts to coordinate with dining area decor.
- Create one unit with open shelving for display of choice objects.

CREATE FANCIFUL LIGHTING

Atmospheric lighting is one of the key ingredients of a memorable meal. Ordinary lighting will do, but by working out special lighting effects, you can transform almost any dining area into a highly inviting place.

Install a Dimmer

You need good lighting to set the table, arrange

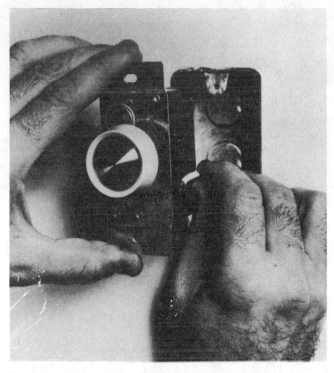

Replace the light switch with a dimmer. (Courtesy of Leviton Manufacturing)

A simple storage cabinet becomes a dramatic focal point through lighting. Deluxe warm white fluorescent tubes located behind the boards highlight both dinnerware and sideboard buffet. (Courtesy of General Electric)

the flatware, and generally tend to the care of the room. Good lighting for these chores, however, is invariably too bright for comfortable dining. In addition, when you light the candles at the table, you alter the total lighting of the room. A dimmer that controls the overhead light or chandelier is a perfect answer to adjusting light to every activity.

Contemporary dimmers come with instructions that make them easy to install; a screwdriver is the only tool you need. Remember to turn off all electricity before making any change such as this.

Light up Treasured Objects

Dining rooms are a natural spot for collections, and collections need to be properly illuminated. You can install simple lighting strips in a humble china cabinet and transform it into a showcase. Take a look at any exposed shelving in your dining area as a possible source for showcase display.

This ceiling dome with a center medallion provides a most impressive custom effect. (Courtesy of Focal Point, Inc.)

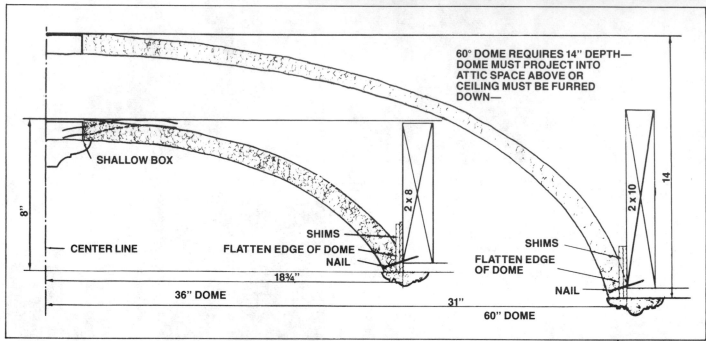

SHALLOW BOX

60° DOME REQUIRES 14" DEPTH—DOME MUST PROJECT INTO ATTIC SPACE ABOVE OR CEILING MUST BE FURRED DOWN—

2 x 8

2 x 10

14

8"

CENTER LINE

SHIMS
FLATTEN EDGE OF DOME
NAIL

SHIMS
FLATTEN EDGE OF DOME

NAIL

18¾"

36" DOME

31"

60" DOME

The dome is anchored by nails to 2 x 8s extending above the ceiling line. First, the edge of the dome is flattened, and shims are used to secure it. Since it is so lightweight, support is not a major problem.

Decorative rims coordinate with cornice moldings. (From Focal Point, Inc.)

Install a Ceiling Dome for a Chandelier

Chandeliers are the obvious problem-solving choices for dining room lighting. They provide the necessary lighting without taking up table room, and with the addition of a dimmer, they can be altered to complement any supplemental lighting.

Since most chandeliers make a very strong design statement for the entire dining room, why not go one better, and decorate the ceiling to enhance that impact? Molding and ceiling decorations can give even the humblest room a feeling of elegance. Besides, a truly handsome chandelier deserves a good background.

A specialty firm called Focal Point, Inc., makes a vast range of authentic reproduction decorative moldings and accessories which are architectural artworks. Made of modern polymers, they are easier to install than multi-member moldings, and resilient enough to conform to minor wall irregularities.

One unique product is a ceiling dome, available in a 3' diameter. It can be installed in existing or new structures. Prior to its introduction, this beautiful way of expanding a room was possible only for those who were able to afford custom wet plaster work. A plaster dome similar to this would weigh several hundred pounds as compared to this one, which weighs a shippable ten pounds.

Three interchangeable decorative rims are available to finish off the dome. These can be coordinated with matching crown molding and accessory strips for use on the walls. Further customizing can be achieved through the use of any 12" x 18" medallion from the company, as a replacement for the standard metal canopy. If your dining room can accommodate it, you may want to use the 5' dome made by Focal Point, Inc. Installation steps are roughly the same for both domes.

Complete instructions come with each dome. The 3' dome can be installed above an existing ceiling with 8" of clearance. The 5' dome requires a 14" depth, so dome must project into the attic space above or the ceiling must be furred down.

The molding, which comes in four sections, is installed with a combination of nails and mastic. Mastic is run in beads along bedding edges of molding. Ends of both pieces at joints are "buttered". Finishing nails are also recommended at either side of joints and at studs. Excess mastic must be removed at once as it is very difficult to remove when cured out, and affects paint or stain finishes. Painting must wait until all mastic is cured, then dome and trim can be painted easily because they are factory-primed white.

Both the molding decorative rims and medallion for the center serve to cover seams. While this dome is not inexpensive, the result is so spectacular that it might be just the ticket for a traditional dining area or even a contemporary one. Focal Point, Inc., also makes a full range of decorative moldings as well as fireplace mantels and stair brackets, with the same true rendition of classic architectural motifs.

CONVENIENT STORAGE AND SERVING

Centerpiece vases, tureens, best silver, dinnerware, glassware, and linens are conveniently stored in the dining room, where they are ready for use. One slick way of garnering space for yourself is to build in a storage wall. Couple this with a tea caddy that goes from kitchen to dining area, and your serving and storage needs are completely taken care of.

Creating a Hidden Storage Wall

The Historic Collection of hardboard paneling from Masonite Corp. recreates some of the wood panel with architectural detailing used in the finest homes in years past. The paneling lends itself to traditional wall application with hidden storage.

Tools and materials. Molding for top and bottom of walls; shelving for inside of storage wall at least 12" deep; contact cement; finishing nails; saw; knobs for doors; bi-fold doors; Provence Masonite paneling; additional lumber to build in storage wall to your specifications.

Steps

1. Plan repeat of matching patterned panels along walls. Measure the wall and mark the center as a starting point. Set up panels. This will enable you to plan the best end patterns. Allow paneling to become acclimated to the room, as per the manufacturer's instructions.

2. After pattern arrangement has been achieved, the first panel can be put into place. Remaining panels are then installed. (Paneling may be installed above existing base molding or old molding may be removed to be reinstalled after paneling is in place.)

3. Follow manufacturer's instructions for installing paneling around windows, doorways, etc., for flat wall applications.

4. *To make concealed storage wall,* start by deciding placement of the doors. Use 16" bi-fold doors, to

Hardboard panels front bi-fold doors along one wall of a dining room. (Courtesy of Masonite Corp., Provence design)

accommodate panels cut lengthwise at 16'' intervals. Plan door placement so that no less than 8'' of a panel width (½ the bi-fold door width) is used at either end. Plan pattern matching, keeping in mind that the concealed storage "wall" adjoins side walls forward from the back wall. Your door pattern design should be incorporated into the most pleasing overall repeating design of the panels as they go around the room.

5. Build up a platform to bring base of the storage area to same height as molding around rest of the room. Make an allowance for channel needed to hold the bi-fold door. Suspend ceiling channel for the bi-fold door from ceiling parallel to the base channel.

6. Install shelving (using one of the systems described in the next chapter). Paint or finish interior of storage area, and install lighting if desired.

7. Use panel adhesive to face the bi-fold doors with panels and allow to set up. Sand, paint, and fill panel edges and bi-fold doors and allow to dry. Apply handles.

8. Apply molding to top and bottom storage wall area (paint if necessary).

9. Install bi-fold doors along storage wall.

10. If you cannot run the bi-fold doors completely along the wall, then create a false mini-wall on which to front the partial paneling section in one or both corners. Use bi-fold manufacturer's instructions for creating the necessary framing.

Make a Buffet/Tea Caddy on Wheels

A serving trolley is a good way of creating a mov-

Two wallpaper patterns set up a kinship, and are separated by a chair rail to create a strong horizontal line. The result: this small area seems larger. (Courtesy of James Seeman Studios)

able feast. Use it for storage and to bring foods from the kitchen into the dining area. Plan its positioning in the dining area near an electrical outlet and you can use it to keep foods warm in electrical chafing dishes or to have hot coffee ready at the meal's end (plans from Georgia-Pacific).

Tools and materials. One panel ½" x 4' x 8' good two sides grade plywood; ½" x ½" x 17' lumber (shelf guides); 3" x ½" x 3' lumber (handles); plastic laminate in one piece 17" x 31" (top), one piece 18" x 14" (shelf), one piece 17" x 14" (optional sliding tray); four casters of 2" diameter; ¾" finishing nails; 1½" finishing nails; waterproof glue; contact cement (for plastic laminate); wood filler; sandpaper; undercoat; semi-gloss enamel.

Steps

1. Cut out parts as per dimensions on illustration.

2. Glue and nail the lower retaining strips (H) flush with the underside of the base (B). Use 1½" nails throughout construction, except for shelf guides.

3. Glue and nail the sides (E) to the base. Mark the dividers (D) for the position of the shelf guides, as shown in the plan. Glue and nail the ½" x ½" shelf guides in position, using ¾" nails.

4. Glue and nail the dividers (D) into position. Make sure the shelf guides are on the inside. Glue and nail the fixed shelf (F) into position as shown. Glue and nail the two upper retaining strips (C) to the sides. Note that these are placed ½" below the top edge.

5. Glue and nail the top (A) to the dividers, sides, and retaining strips. Glue and nail handles at both ends. Attach casters to base.

6. The plan allows one adjustable shelf (G). Ad-

A buffet on wheels is as appropriate outdoors as it is inside. This modular unit can be finished to coordinate with any decor. (Courtesy of Georgia-Pacific)

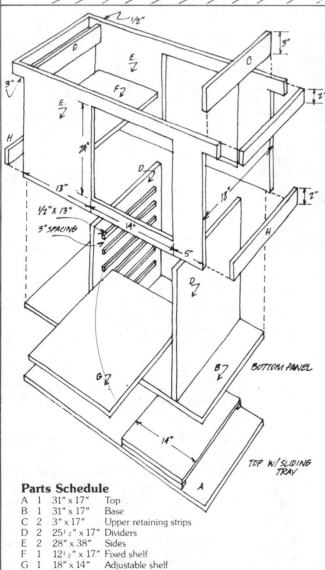

ditional shelves can be made from ½'' plywood if you wish.

7. Countersink all nails. Fill nail holes and all exposed plywood edges with wood filler. Sand edges and filled areas, then paint all surfaces with white primer except those to be covered with plastic laminate. Sand lightly and apply second undercoat, tinted with the desired finish color. Sand again, then paint with one or more coats of semi-gloss enamel.

8. Apply the plastic laminate to the top and adjustable shelves with contact cement. If preferred, this can be applied to the top before it is set in place.

9. The sliding top tray, which serves to hold glasses and dishes in place, is optional. It can be made from ½'' plywood, 17'' x 14'', with ½'' x ½'' strips for the runners. The top can be painted or covered with plastic laminate.

Parts Schedule

A	1	31'' x 17''	Top
B	1	31'' x 17''	Base
C	2	3'' x 17''	Upper retaining strips
D	2	25½'' x 17''	Dividers
E	2	28'' x 38''	Sides
F	1	12½'' x 17''	Fixed shelf
G	1	18'' x 14''	Adjustable shelf
H	2	2'' x 17''	Lower retaining strips

7
Family Room Projects

That relic-filled basement or cluttered extra room may have been the start of your family room, but with custom effects and do-it-yourself furnishings, you can convert it into a showcase. Personal family touches belong in the family room more than in any other room, so don't hold back on them. Your own inventive efforts will add immeasurably to the character that makes any family room decor successful.

Projects and plans in this chapter cover casual suggestions, as well as ideas for more elegant family recreation rooms. Included are accent wall treatments, window ideas, shelving systems, a storage closet, tables, plant accessories, artwork to make, tips on picture groupings, and simple custom floor treatments.

MAKE WALLS DRAMATIC

Dramatic walls transform ordinary spaces. They are especially impressive in basements that are converted into family rooms. The least expensive approach is to make only one wall an accent wall, and to paint the other walls to coordinate with the accent wall. You may find, however, that totally decorating all four walls gives your room distinction. The choice is yours.

Installing Diagonal Paneling

Soaring diagonal paneling, diamond patterns, and other variations that fill the entire wall space are far more interesting than conventional vertical paneling. While more complicated to install and fit than the usual methods for an accent wall, the impressive end result is well worth the effort.

New, light-weight woodstrips are available that can be cut with a utility knife or shears to create your unique designs. You apply them directly over flat wall surfaces suitable for application of wall-covering, but with more adhesion for rougher surfaces than wallcovering offers. The woodstrips are sold in packages to cover 33 square feet of surface area. Various lengths from 1' to 4' are included in the packages to give a varied planked effect (directions adapted from Pope and Talbot).

Tools and materials. Woodstrip packages to cover (plus 10 percent additional for waste); straightedge; shears; utility knife; paneling adhesive (about two tubes per package); caulking gun; masking tape; stain (optional); sealer; brush.

Steps

1. Sketch a condensed form of your pattern on paper, then try layout of a few test pieces. Each package has dark heartwood and light sapwood, with surface texture ranging from smooth to brushy grain. Vary the light and dark strips in the most pleasing manner, and stagger adjacent joints.

2. Forty-five degree angles for diagonal installations are most versatile, because they will butt up easily with right-angled side walls, and they prevent unnecessary cutting of odd angles. A triangle will guide you in making true 45 degree cuts.

3. Prepare surface to be covered, making sure that it is free of grease and soil and relatively smooth. Prime if necessary as you would for wallcovering.

4. Prepare a clean area of the floor for working out your layout. Mask off area of wall to be covered and place strips into position, starting from the bottom section of wall layout. (If wall is large, you may want to lay out bottom few feet in this way, making sure contrast between strips is attractive.)

5. To cut strips, use one of two methods. With a utility knife, mark the line you want to cut on the strip,

Diagonal paneling creates a contemporary but soft background for handsome, modern knockdown furniture. (Courtesy of James David, Inc.)

Easy-to-install woodstrips come in a variety of natural grains and colors. (Courtesy of Pope and Talbot, Inc.)

toward the point or center of the strip. Another method is to mark the strip and use shears to cut it.

6. For small pieces (shorter than 5'') used in a corner or hard-to-fit spot, cover the back side of the piece with masking tape, and cut through the tape. This avoids splintering. Leave the tape on the back and just glue over the tape.

7. Start applying strips at the bottom, so they will not slide down before paneling adhesive sets up. If you must start at the top, use staples to help hold strips in place. After the adhesive has dried, carefully remove the staples.

8. Before applying any glue, check the fit of each piece. You may have to trim away excess wood if measurement was not exact. Be sure to butt each row as closely as possible to the next.

9. Apply adhesive to the back of each strip. Cut the nozzle tip of the caulking gun applicator so the hole is approximately 1/8'' in diameter. Run a long nail or wire into the nozzle to break the plastic seal. Hold the tube at a slight angle to the surface of the wood to allow the glue to flow out evenly. Squeeze a bead around the perimeter on the back of each strip, and then add a few dashes down the middle of the strip to assure uniform coverage. Apply adhesive sparingly so it will not ooze out.

10. Use a gentle, back-and-forth sliding action to apply the strips to the surface. Unwanted glue that may seep out from behind strips during compression can be cut or peeled off after glue has dried. Check occasionally to make sure strips haven't lifted or shifted.

11. For a complete wall, you can stain strips after they are applied. When more than one color is used, or you are working in a small area, you can stain individual strips before adhering (but remember to allow them to dry thoroughly before gluing).

12. You can leave wood unfinished. But either with stains or without added color, it is advisable to use a sealer, especially around high moisture areas and much used areas such as light switches. Apply stain or sealer with a brush.

Variations

• Make adventurous patterns such as diamonds, combinations of horizontal and

5. To cut strips, use one of two methods. With a utility knife, mark the line you want to cut on the strip, place a metal straightedge over the line, and bear down to steady it. With the utility knife in your other hand, cut along the marked-off line, using the metal straightedge as a guide. Always cut at the side of the strip with the grain, going

Conventional stucco takes on a dramatic flavor when covered with a reflecting enamel in a dark color. The light fairly dances on the surfaces. (Courtesy of James David, Inc.)

A bold random-texture pattern forms the perfect background for treasured art objects. (Courtesy of United States Gypsum Co.)

vertical application, or patchwork patterns with the strips.

• Use conventional planking or plywood with regular grooves to cover a wall diagonally. Investigate taller lengths of plywood (such as 4' x 10') to eliminate seaming. You can cover seams with molding if necessary, and for added decorative effect.

Make a Textured Wall

Painted or plain white, stucco walls are dramatic. You can create a unique surface by applying stucco or textured paint, and texturing with burlap, rope, or other textured pieces.

Textured paints come in various degrees of thickness, allowing for light through heavy textured effects. All have the advantage of mitigating surface imperfections, such as cracks or joints. Some are specifically designed to go directly over cement block; others are designed for use over conventional walls.

The heavier textured paints are the more interesting to work with, and allow for greatest textural creativity. Think twice about the application of a heavily textured surface to a wall before putting it up, because it is extremely difficult to change once installed. With this in mind, decide whether you want to texturize all four walls or use a paint surface on three, leaving the texturing to the accent wall.

Here are some inventive textured effects suggested by United States Gypsum Co., which produces textured paints.

—Apply paint with a trowel, then finish in an intriguing arc pattern with a texture brush, creating a random swirled effect.

—Create a bold random-texture pattern by using a notched trowel in short strokes in many directions.

—Press wet burlap into freshly applied texturing material for an unusual antique effect.

—Use a long-nap roller to create moderate surface texture in a relatively quick application.

—Create wavelike effects with simple brush texturing in gentle arcs that overlap.

118

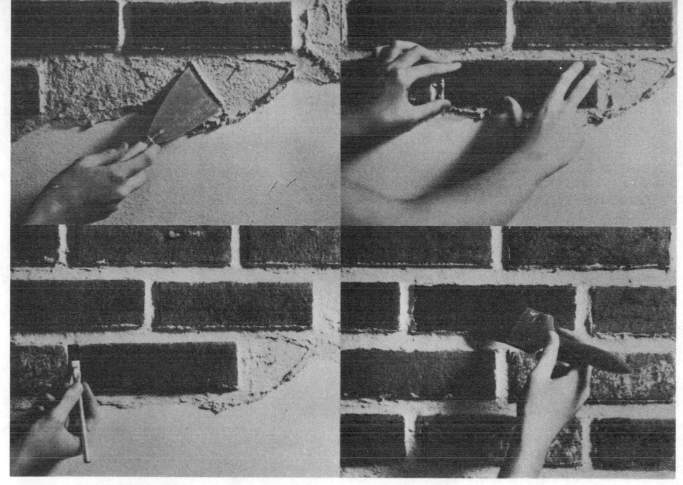

Lightweight Z-Brick installs in four easy steps: apply cement adhesive mortar; press brick into place; smooth mortar joint with a narrow brush; apply non-glossy Z-Sealer.

—Make a cross-hatch texture that reflects the rustic charm of rural America by pressing a wooden strip into the damp surface of the paint, first vertically, then horizontally.

—Use a wooden square to impress a repeat geometric pattern on the wall. Overlap the squares and run them in lines, either horizontally or vertically.

—Use rope wrapped around a roller to create a naturalistic texture that is impressed with the rope imprint. Work across the wall with the roller for horizontal ridges.

—Use a wide-toothed comb to create circular swirls that are closely spaced. Merely rotate the comb in a tight circle.

—Use favorite natural objects, such as leaves, shells, or branches, to create an almost fossilized effect with your wall covering.

Tools and materials. Paint; trowel for applying; tints for tinting textured paint or paint for finish coating; special texturing tool (such as comb); drop cloth.

Steps

1. Repair any gross cracks in the wall surface and remove any grease or dust from wall. Cover floor.

2. Experiment with your texturing technique on a small wall section. An old piece of wallboard works nicely. Make sure you have the technique mastered before applying textured wall paint to the wall.

3. Follow manufacturer's instructions for applying and finishing wall. In most cases, it is suggested that you start on the least dominant section of the wall, covering a section with the textured paint and texturing that section as you go along. Manufacturer's directions will give you the set-up time so that you can gauge the amount of wall that can be conveniently covered and then textured before it becomes too dry for working.

4. Remember to stand back and survey your work as you go along to catch any repeat patterns that should not appear in an all-over random design.

5. Allow ample time for the wall to dry before using the room.

Variation: Brick Wall

Brick walls are good accent walls for contemporary or traditional family rooms. A brick wall is a traditional

119

Natural Belgian linen wallcovering creates an interesting textural effect and is a subtle background for furnishings. (Courtesy of Belgian Linen Association)

background for a free-standing fireplace, affording both beauty and practicality. Check to see that your choice of brick or imitation brick is fireproof, to give added protection.

Lightweight imitation bricks are easy to install, and do not burden the floor with as heavy a weight as a real brick wall does. You can find imitation bricks in a number of colors and degrees of antiquity; corner and end pieces make joinings easy, and once installed, they are hard to tell from the real thing.

Other suggestions for textured walls: install fieldstone imitation stones for walls, or use a combination of stucco or textured paint plus scattered bricks to create a peasant-farm effect. You may wish to use brickwork solely on the section of wall that is directly behind a firestove. Or you may create an artificial fireplace front for looks alone.

Cover Walls With Fabric

Fabric makes an attractive wallcovering for an accent wall or for an entire room. It is especially good for decorating walls that are imperfect, and it helps deaden some sound. These simple steps (suggested by the Belgian Linen Association) make it easy to put up fabrics with a staple gun.

Make a plan of the room to scale on paper, measuring wall areas and including doors and windows. Divide plan into exact width of fabric exclusive of selvage. Lay out fabric face up to decide on pattern repeat at ceiling and to make sure each panel matches. Cut into matching strips allowing an extra 2" for fold-in on both top and bottom. (Use smaller pieces around windows, etc.)

Tools and materials. Sufficient material to cover the wall; trim for ceiling and baseboard seam; hand staple gun or automatic stapler which may be rented; cardboard or wood strips cut 1" x 1/8" and 1/16"; hammer and small nails; sharp scissors; sharp fabric knife; folding ruler; plumb line; pliers to remove nail heads; ladder; glue for trim.

BRINGING THE OUTDOORS INSIDE

Family rooms, especially those located in the basement, notoriously suffer from a lack of windows. There is no need to comply with the real surroundings if you want to open up the space. Through clever use of window and wall coverings, you can create your own spaciousness, with images of vistas, in the most subterranean cavern.

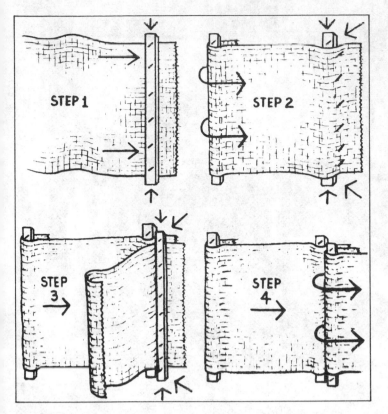

Make a plan of the room to scale on paper, measuring wall areas and including doors and windows. Divide plan into exact width of fabric exclusive of selvage. Lay out fabric face up to decide on pattern repeat at ceiling and to make sure each panel matches. Cut into matching strips allowing an extra 2" for fold-in on both top and bottom. (Use smaller pieces around windows, etc.)

1. It is easiest to start in the left corner. Hold the fabric inside out with all but 1" at left of starting point. Place thicker cardboard vertically on fabric, and push up into the corner. Place staples 2" apart top to bottom on cardboard strip to anchor left edge of fabric. If starting away from the corner, use a plumb line to place cardboard vertically on fabric and staple.

2. Pull fabric taut from left to right for location of next cardboard at right edge of fabric. Staple thicker cardboard to wall 1" in from right side of pattern edge, underneath, not on the fabric. Stretch fabric across this second cardboard and staple it firmly top and bottom.

3. Place next width of fabric on first piece, matching pattern at left edge. Anchor with three staples at top. Stretch to bottom and fasten with staples, taking care to match pattern exactly. Push thin cardboard strip up against strip already installed. Match pattern by stretching fabric as strip is stapled down.

4. Continue with this method for length of walls. For final panel, stretch fabric full width, trim 2" wider than space to be covered. Fold fabric over heavy cardboard and press into right-hand corner. Slip back to tighten and tack down with small nails. Hammer small nails halfway in, cut off heads with pliers, and hammer until flush with fabric. Window and doorway openings are treated by stapling heavy cardboard around opening. Fabric is drawn taut, then stapled into place close to edge. Use a sharp knife to remove excess fabric, then cover staples with molding or braid.

Create False Windows

You will not lose much wall space by building out a wall to accommodate false windows. You will create a feeling of spaciousness, even though these windows were never meant to be opened (suggestion from Levelor Blinds).

Tools and materials. Wallboard to create modernistic floor-to-ceiling window frames; a fluorescent light to install at the base of each window frame; floor-to-ceiling blinds.

Steps

1. Create simple, streamlined window frames, built out about 1' from existing wall. Recess sides about 2" in from frames.

2. Install fluorescent lamps across the bottom of the window space, at the back. Paint back wall white for reflection.

3. Install floor-to-ceiling window shades, allowing 1" on either side to be clear. Shades are placed about 4" back from front of frame.

4. Use light, reflective shades for the greatest illusion of space. Turn shades slightly, so that light behind them spills through and around the sides. The added touch of plants furthers the illusion of greenery on the other side of the shade.

Extend a Small Window

Here is an inexpensive means of visually expanding a typical basement window (plans from *1,001 Decorating Ideas*).

Tools and materials. Shutters; lattice stripping; ¼" plywood; mirror; paint for frames.

Steps

1. Cut a mirror two times as tall as the window, and the same width as the window. Mount it to matching plywood backing with 1" of plywood border around the sides, ½" border at top.

2. Place lattice stripping to simulate window frame, dividing mirror into four panes and framing entire mirror "window". Attach to plywood, and mount entire unit below real window.

3. Extend matching stripping around real window to achieve continuity if necessary.

4. Attach shutters extending length of window and false window.

No dark and gloomy basement walls here. These false windows with backlighting and plants in front bring nature into the home. Sleek Venetian blinds are essential to this handsome illusion, or try adding a handsome lambrequin. (Courtesy of Levelor Blinds)

Another eye-fooling window trick is extending a small basement window with the use of mirrors. (Courtesy of 1,001 Decorating Ideas)

This light-hearted furniture is hefty enough to be comfortable for indoor seating, but maintains an airiness that keeps the room "outdoors" in spirit. (From Thayer Coggin, designed by Milo Baughman)

Make a Gazebo Effect with Latticework

Latticework on the walls can transform a room into an outdoor gazebo. Follow through with a color scheme in yellows and greens; add plenty of white and wicker.

Tools and materials for walls. Level; wire and weight for plumb line; lattice stripping; nails (or staples); white paint.

Steps

1. Paint background walls.

2. Starting from ceiling line, attach lattice strips horizontally, 6'' on center. Use level to check trueness.

3. Using same 6'' on center spacing, nail vertical strips to horizontal lattice strips, starting in corner. Use a plumb line to make sure strips are true vertical.

Variations

- Use lattice stripping on only one wall.
- Use lattice stripping to cover ceiling as well as walls.
- Use lattice stripping to outline specific architectural features, such as a wet bar area, door frames, or windows.

Use an Outdoor Scene to Cover Wall

Fabulous graphics, realistic down to the last leaf, are available for creating a panorama on a wall. They are installed in much the same way as conventional wallcoverings, a panel at a time (directions from Environmental Graphics).

Tools and materials. Photo mural panels (finished measure, 8'6'' x 13'8''); package of cellulose or dextrine adhesive so graphic can be stripped off; container in which to mix adhesives; paste brush; newspapers or drop cloth; container with clear water and sponge for after-hanging clean-up; smoothing brush for applying panels; chalk line or level; stepladder; seam roller, straightedge ruler with flat edge or broad knife for trimming if needed; single-edge razor blades.

Steps

1. Prepare the wall. Countersink nails, fill holes, etc., as you would in applying conventional wallcovering. Use a primer-sealer to prevent show-through over a previously painted surface. Remove electrical outlet covers, vents, etc.

2. Make a layout. Graphics come in panels, half on top and half on bottom. Decide how you want to center important features to go with wall protuberances such as doors or windows, if necessary. Determine best positioning of mural on your wall by starting in the center of the graphic and working toward either end.

3. Inspect graphic for shading and design match by laying it out. Imperfect murals can be returned, but not after you have put them on the wall.

4. Mark a true vertical chalk line where you intend to place the first panels on the wall.

5. Start your pasting procedure. Set up an area on floor or table where you can apply paste to graphic. Use formula for "heavy wall coverings" in mixing paste, and mix until all lumps are dissolved. Apply paste to all back area of panel, and "book" panel, folding to center but without creasing. Set panel aside to relax for a minimum of fifteen minutes, to allow for expansion and contraction. Several panels at a time may be booked, loosely rolled, and set aside in this manner.

6. Apply panels. Start with the top panel, overlapping onto ceiling or molding according to how high you want the center of the design. With the edge of the panel in position along plumb line, push bubbles and wrinkles out with the smoothing brush. Eliminate large bubbles or wrinkles by pulling back corner and smoothing again. Small bubbles and wrinkles disappear as material contracts during drying. If wrinkles will not come out, it is an indication that paste has begun to dry or panels are incorrectly positioned. Repaste and rehang.

   Most important: do not stretch the panel or treat it roughly, or it will not line up correctly.

7. Apply bottom panel, matching it up with registration marks as guides only. Slight mismatching will not be visible from a distance.

8. Line up adjacent panels with first panels, and complete wall.

9. To finish, trim excess at baseboard or floor overlap and at ceiling line. Seal all overlapped seams with the seam roller. Lightly wipe down entire area, using a wet sponge to remove any paste from surfaces, especially along seams.

Contact your local photo-graphic supply house for ways of transforming your own creative pictures into a photomural. Apply the mural in sections much as the manufactured ones, and coat with special lacquer for a truly custom look. (Eastman Kodak Co. room designed by Richard W. Jones, FASID)

A forest can bloom on the wall of your own home. So can other realistic murals, or re-productions of artists' works. (Photo courtesy of Scandecor)

Check with your local photographer for decorative shots that he can print to any specified size, and use outdoor scenes such as these skiing pictures to set off a bookcase. (Courtesy of Eastman Kodak Co.)

10. Double-cut overlapped seams if necessary, using razor blades and a straightedge such as a long, flat metal ruler. Take care not to stretch seam. Double-cut by cutting through both over-lapped panels at once, about $1/16$" to $1/8$" from edge. Remove inner and outer excess trim, and carefully push edges together so that there is a very small excess of material at butt joint. Reseal with seam roller, lightly repaste edges and reset with seam roller if necessary.

Shelves that fill in and around your furniture arrangements look totally customed. These were secured to frames with dado grooves. (Room by Richard W. Jones for Eastman Kodak Co.)

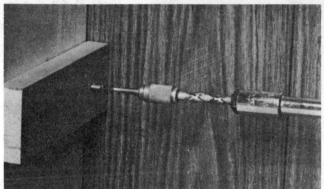

Cleats cut out of furring strips or scrap wood make good shelf supports. (Courtesy of Stanley Tools)

Easy-To-Make Shelving

One of these shelving systems is bound to solve your problems for storage of books, records, or games (systems suggested by Stanley Tools). Remember that if shelves are longer than 36'', you need to add an additional support in the middle.

Cleat supports

This is an easy means of installing shelves between a wall and nearby partition, or within a framework.

Tools and materials. 1'' x 2'' or 1'' x 3'' furring strips or scraps (two per shelf cut slightly shorter than shelf); wood screwdriver; carpenter's level; flathead screws; shelves.

Steps

1. Mount a cleat (furring strip) at each end using at least two flathead screws, using the level to make sure that the shelf is properly aligned and that cleats are at the same height.

2. If installing many shelves, consider getting a Yankee spiral-ratchet screwdriver to ease the chore considerably.

3. Lay shelves on cleats.

4. Paint cleats and shelves to match. Finish by placing molding along sides of unit to hide cleats.

Dowels

Dowels provide a more elegant way than cleats for installing shelves between a wall and partition or within a frame.

Tools and materials. Half-inch hardwood dowels, two per side per shelf; brace and auger bit for an electric drill with a power bore bit; shelves; level.

Steps

1. Drill a ½'' hole just part way into the uprights at each side, recessed about 1'' from front and back

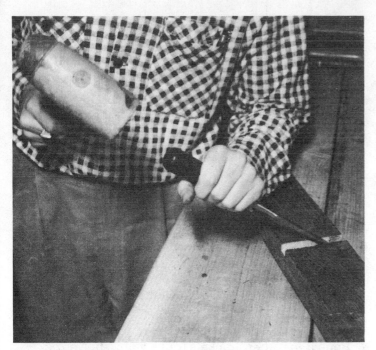

Utilizing dados in shelf construction insures sturdy, permanent and professional results. (Courtesy of Stanley Tools)

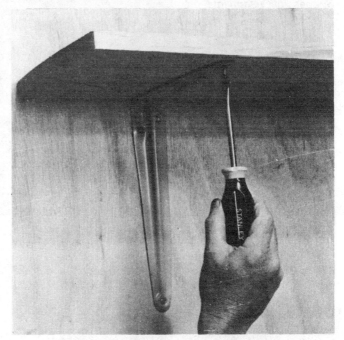

Steel shelf brackets are used when a shelf cannot be supported at either end. (Courtesy of Stanley Tools)

of shelf. Cut dowels so that they will stick out 1'' from holes when inserted.

2. Use level to make sure holes are positioned properly.

3. Lay shelves on dowels. To move shelves, drill new holes and move dowels to new position.

Dados

Dados are grooves cut across the width of a board that must be equal to the width in thickness of the shelf it will support. By creating dados in the end boards of a shelf unit, you can create sturdy, permanent shelves. While more complicated than cleats or dowels, the results look more professional.

Tools and materials. Workbench; end boards or frame; straight piece of hardwood; chisel; carpenter's ruler; shelves; glue; nails.

Steps

1. Carefully measure along length of two boards and mark where shelf dados are to be made.

2. Clamp end board to a work bench and also clamp a straight piece of hardwood even with the pencil line of the dado cut.

3. Begin by making a few passes over the middle of the cut to get the feel of the work. Carefully cut a partial depth of ⅛'' to ¼'' to prevent overshooting

and splintering later.

4. Start at the near end and hold the chisel between 45 and 60 degrees. Move back and forth across the dado.

5. Keep the dado free from chips. Glue and set dado joint. You can further reinforce by nailing through side board through end of shelf. Repeat for other side and all shelves.

6. Finish front edge of unit with molding to cover dado joints.

Brackets

Brackets attached directly to the wall give an open feeling to shelving.

Tools and materials. Brackets or angle brackets; masonry fasteners; nails; shelving; level. Brackets come in many sizes to support shelves up to 12'' wide.

Steps

1. Find the wall studs for secure placement of brackets. Mount wall brackets with the short leg under the shelf and long leg on the wall. Secure brackets, spaced as wanted, along one side.

2. Position brackets on other side, using a level to make sure shelf will be level before securing bracket.

3. To prevent the shelf from shifting, secure shelf to the bracket. Use flathead screws with angle brackets. For extra heavy loads, use two angle brackets at each end of shelf.

Bird's Mouth Brackets

This triangular wooden support can be plain or fancy.

Tools and materials. Scrap wood or 1'' x 3'' furring strips; nails; miter box; level; shelves.

Bracket holders are slotted at 1'' spaces to accommodate for adjustments at any time. (Courtesy of Stanley Tools)

Steps

1. Cut a 45 degree notch into horizontal member that is slightly shorter than shelf width (this is called a bird's mouth joint).

2. Cut long vertical strip to be at rear on wall, and nail horizontal member to it through top end of wall strip.

3. Cut a diagonal strut at a 45 degree miter on *one* end so that it fits into bird's mouth joint at top, and mitered end rests on upright strip.

4. Secure upright strip and horizontal strip to wall, nailing or screwing into studs.

5. Place top end of diagonal strip into bird's mouth joint, and nail bottom mitered end to upright strip secured to wall.

6. Repeat for other brackets for as many shelves as necessary, making sure that shelves are level before securing completely.

Bracket standards

One of the most versatile forms of free-standing shelving uses a bracket standard and holders. These come in a variety of finishes to suit your decor, and can be painted.

Tools and materials. Bracket standards with slotted spaces; brackets to fit bracket standards; shelving; level; fastening for mounting bracket standards to wall, such as screws.

A bird's mouth joint at top and a miter cut at the bottom are used to make this shelf support. (Courtesy of Stanley Tools)

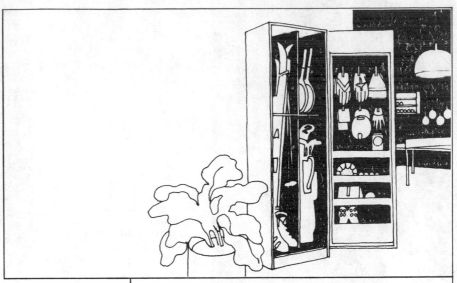

This handsome and rugged unit can hide a multitude of sports equipment, or anything else you wish. (Plans courtesy of Georgia-Pacific)

Steps

1. Find stud and mount one side bracket strip. Allow one foot of bracket above top shelf so that weight will be well distributed along standard.

2. Position brackets along length of standard. Often, a tap at the bracket base with a hammer will secure it into standard.

3. Use a shelf or board and level to make sure that second standard is attached to wall at the same level. Slots on either side must be at the same height for shelves to stay level.

Make a Storage Cabinet

Here is a storage cabinet perfect for sports gear, sewing and cleaning tools, and almost any bulky items (plans from Georgia-Pacific).

Tools and materials. Two panels ¾'' x 4' x 8' Exterior good two sides plywood; one piece ¼'' x 3' x 8' exterior good one side plywood; 2½' of ½'' quarter-round nailing strip; 1 lb. of 1½'' finishing nails, 1 lb. of 2'' finishing nails; glue; wood filler; one door bolt; four pin hinges; one ¾'' hinge for drop bar; clothes pins as required; paint as required; good saw.

Steps

1. Cut cabinet parts on three panels, remembering to allow for the width of the saw cuts and space between the parts (use ¼'' plywood for back and shelf parts).

2. Mark the parts for identification and sand edges that will show.

3. Rabbet one end of each side panel for the top. Assemble the cabinet back-side down on the floor, using glue and finishing nails.

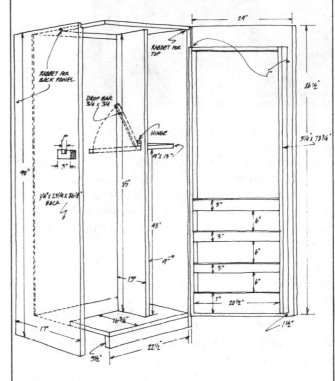

4. Install drop bars made from ½'' quarter round on division in cabinet.

5. Assemble the door framing strips on the door panel, then add the shelves and facing strips. Nail clothes pins to door to hold hanging items.

6. Attach the door with the four pin hinges, add bolt, and finish as desired.

Variations

- Hang a mirror or mirror tiles to outside of the unit.
- Cover with self-stick or other wallcovering.

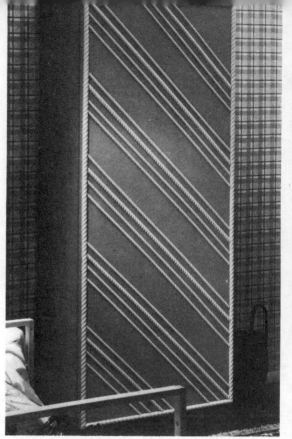

Now you see it, now you don't. With clever decorative molding on the outside, this storage cabinet is handsome enough to become the focal point on a wall. (Molding from Klise, wallcovering from J. Josephson)

WINE STORAGE UNITS

Wine storage units incorporated into a living room can add elegance as well as a practical touch. Here are some suggestions from a Louisiana-Pacific booklet of wine rack construction plans. The booklet covers virtually any design you might want to make.

Six-Bottle Rack

This portable wine rack has a clean, simple design. The rack looks attractive standing on its own; it can also be tucked away on shelves. It is 9" deep, 18" wide, and 12" high.

Tools and materials. Two pieces redwood, 1" x 12" x 18" for front and back; four oak or birch ¾" x 9" dowels; coping, jig, or saber saw; ¼" drill; ¾" drill; glue.

Modern Rounded Wine Box

This rounded-corners unit can be used horizontally or vertically. The box is constructed to hold together cylinders that in turn hold the bottles. The wine box can perch on a countertop or serve as an end table.

Tools and materials. Two pieces redwood, 2" x 12" x 20¼" for top and bottom; two pieces redwood, 2" x 12" x 12¼" for sides; one piece ⅜" x 14" x 19" particleboard or plywood for back; twelve dowels, ¾" x 3"; twelve fiberboard cylinders, 4" x 10" (often found in carpet stores, cut to size); ¾" drill, nails, sandpaper, plane, and wood rasp; glue; finishing materials.

You may alter the overall dimensions of the box to fit cylinders of a slightly different size, but no smaller than 4" inside diameter. Cylinders can be purchased at modest cost for elegant touch.

Ideas for Cylinders

Sources for free cylinders include 46 oz. fruit juice cans with tops and bottoms removed. The cans may be spraypainted a decorative color. Another source is fiberboard cores around which rug or carpeting is rolled. These tubes are usually free for the asking from local carpet stores. Trim the tube to proper length, sand the edges, and finish with paint or a clear sealer.

Inexpensive cylinders can be created from heavy duty mailing tubes usually available at stationery stores at nominal cost. More expensive cylinders that are very handsome include plastic drain or clay field tile pipes. Use epoxy glue to fasten this material together.

General Wine Storage Tips

Whatever wine storage system you use, here are some good tips for keeping your wines in good con-

1. Drill ¾" holes through top and bottom pieces and into side pieces. Assemble box and glue joints.
2. Apply back for stiffening, nailing around sides.
3. Trim corners at a 45 degree angle and round to 1⅝" with plane, wood rasp, and sandpaper.
4. Insert and glue cylinders into place (prepaint cylinder if desired).
5. Sand carefully and finish as desired.

1. Round all corners on redwood pieces to a 2" radius.
2. Lay out 4" diameter circles approximately 5" on center and cut out. (Drill starting hole and use saw to cut out holes.)
3. Drill ¾" holes in each corner about 1" in from edges for dowels.
4. Insert dowels and glue in place. Sand carefully and finish.

dition until the very moment they are ready for enjoying. The more wine you plan to store, the more important it is that your storage be good for the wine itself. Many contemporary wines do not need the coddling of days past, but here are the general guidelines to follow.

Light. Strong light, especially sunlight, can be harmful to wine if a bottle is exposed for long periods. It is not necessary to reproduce sealed darkroom conditions, but all wines should be protected from light as much as possible. This is the reason why many white wines are often packaged in dark green or brown bottles.

Vibration. Wines should rest quietly. Constant vibration can damage flavor, so avoid storage near washers, dryers, dishwashers, refrigerators, and other machinery with vibrating motors.

Temperature. Extreme and frequent fluctuations in temperature are to be avoided. Wines may be safely stored for years in a fairly stable temperature ranging from 50 to 70 degrees. Temperatures are cooler at floor level and on interior walls or closets, rather than on exterior walls subject to sunlight and daily temperature changes. Store wines in the cooler areas. Position wine racks away from heat sources such as water heaters, stoves, and heat ducts.

Placement. Wine racks should be designed so bottles will rest on sides, keeping the corks moist. Dry corks allow air to enter the bottle and spoil contents. The only exceptions to this rule of horizontal storage are bottles sealed with plastic corks or metal screw caps, which may be safely stored upright. Horizontal rack designs should allow air to circulate and when possible, permit each bottle to be removed without disturbing its neighbor.

Bulk Wine Storage Systems—Wall Racks

One of the most attractive ways to display and store your wines is to create either an entire wine rack wall or to create an accent wine wall section. Many of the units designed for small quantity storage are adaptable to larger numbers of bottles with the simple addition of shelving to accommodate them. Keep in mind that more bottles mean more weight, which demands heavier material and more solid fastening systems. For heavy storage, wood or lag screws or nut and bolt fasteners should be used rather than nails.

Here are some suggestions for making "wine storage walls."

Basic squares. Repeat a basic bulk storage module of squares of 14" inner dimension by 12" deep. Alternate flat and standing bottles in the squares.

Shelves and cylinders. Construct heavy-duty shelves tall enough to take two alternating rows of cylinders. Add supports a minimum of every 24", spaced to hold the cylinders snug on the bottom row. Glue cylinders to one another. Use the cylinders suggested for the small wine box.

Diamond Wall. Create square modules with shelving 12" deep within a frame, but set at a 45 degree angle. The diamond pattern allows for storage for less than case quantities in individual sections, especially if each section is designed to take nine bottles. Add several horizontal shelves inserted in the diamond to store glasses and cork screws. The rack can be constructed floor to ceiling, but to avoid unnecessary vibration should *not* be attached directly to floor joist above.

Shelves and diagonal dividers. Add diagonal dividers set at 30 degree angles alternately to shelves 12" deep. Create a frame to fill a space from floor to ceiling, wall to wall, or within a closet.

Understairs storage. Dress up the unused area beneath stairs by converting it into a wine cellar. Use a simple 2 x 4 framework to support front and rear racks, cut out to accommodate bottle ends and necks. Allow at least 14" from the bottom shelf to the floor so that full cases or gallon bottles may be stored here. Attach rack firmly to wall or floor; however, to avoid excess vibrations, do *not* attach to stairs.

SPECIAL TABLES

Here are plans for a hostess table and some clever ideas for dressing up traditional Parson's tables and cubes. One is bound to suit your family room.

Hostess Table and Seating Cubes

This project combines a low table, perfect for serving snacks or drinks, and seats to provide extra seating for a party. Seats tuck under the table to save space when they are not in use. And, by removing the seat tops, you have storage space for toys, papers, or games (plans from Georgia-Pacific).

Hostess Table & Seating Cubes

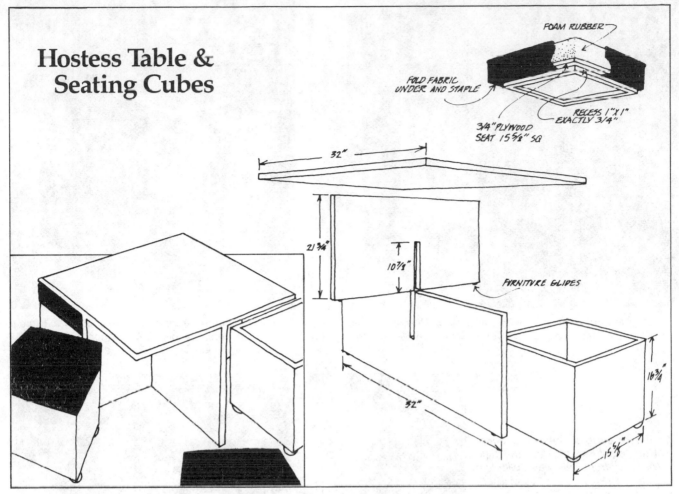

FOAM RUBBER

FOLD FABRIC UNDER AND STAPLE

¾" PLYWOOD SEAT 15⅝" SQ

RECESS 1" X 1" EXACTLY ¾"

32"

21¾"

10⅞"

FURNITURE GLIDES

32"

16¾"

15⅝"

1. Mark out and cut the individual pieces from the two sheets of ¾" plywood, using good two sides plywood for table. Remember to allow for the width of the saw cut when marking.
2. Use a chisel to make the end cut in the two matching slots in the table base, centered on pieces. Assemble the base by mating the slots.
3. Attach table top with glue and 2" finishing nails. Fasten nylon furniture glides to four corners of the base as shown.
4. For each seat box, butt join corners of sides, and fasten with glue and 2" finishing nails. Attach bottom (same size as seat) with glue and finishing nails.
5. Nail four strips of 1" x 1" molding under where seat will be, exactly ¾" in from top edges so seat will fit snugly into the box base.

6. Make upholstery covers for the seat cushions, allowing at least 2" of fabric below the bottom of the cushion. Fasten the cushion to the plywood seat by folding the fabric underneath and stapling or tacking it.
7. Attach casters to box bottoms. Make sure casters do not protrude beyond box sides and prevent the seats from fitting snugly under the table.
8. Before painting, countersink the nails and fill the holes and all exposed plywood edges with wood filler. Sand the edges and filled areas, then apply a coat of primer. Sand lightly and apply a second coat of primer tinted with the desired finish color. Sand again and finish with one or more coats of semi-gloss enamel.

Tools and materials. One panel ¾" x 4' x 8' Exterior good two sides plywood; one panel ¾" x 4' x 8' Exterior good one side plywood; 1" x 1" x 16' s4s lumber; 16 shepherd casters (plate-type base with screws); upholstery fabric; staples or tacks; four foam rubber slabs (15⅝" square x 2" thick); four furniture glides (⅝" diameter); 1 lb. of 2" finishing nails; chisel; glue; wood filler; paint or stain.

Variations

• Cover the cubes with fabric to match the seating.

• Paint each different chair/stool a different color.

Special Decorations for Tables

Here are some easy suggestions for dressing up either Parson's or cube tables. Use tables you make yourself from directions in this book, or ready-made unpainted pieces.

Mirrored table. This is a good substantial storage/coffee table cube that has the look of lightness. Box dimensions are 2' square by 1' high (add casters if

133

Any decorative molding with character will transform an ordinary Parson's table. (Courtesy of Klise Manufacturing Co.)

Favorite photographs can make an end table into a conversation piece. (Designed by Richard W. Jones, FASID, for Eastman Kodak Co.)

A handsome rug deserves repeating. Here, a coffee table does the trick. (Area rug from Callaway Collection by Milliken)

you wish). Cover the exterior of the sides with self-stick mirror tiles, and top with grasscloth. Use glue to attach a decorative molding where top and sides join.

Picture cube. This end table also doubles as storage. Decorate the table with square photographs directly mounted to the painted wooden surface of the table. Frames surround the pictures and are made of molding trim.

Dressed-up Parson's. The molding added to the legs, apron, and top of this simple Parson's table make it unique. Choose molding that matches the mood of your family room to make a similar accessory. As a

miniature game table, a unit decorated with molding has the added advantage of assuring no lost checkers or chessmen.

PLANNING FOR PLANTS

The lush green of plants is often the best decorative touch you can add to a room. In a family room, particularly one that started as a converted basement with little outside view, plants cut through any feelings of claustrophobia. Here are some guidelines for creating appropriate home plant atmospheres, and for creating interesting planters. Green thumbing is left strictly up to you.

134

Decorative grills disguise the overhead lights that keep these window plants blooming. Hanging planters can be attached to the grilles, so that plants can be arranged at will. (Courtesy of DuroLite)

Lighting

Lighting is critical to the growth and health of indoor plants. These pointers describe the best surroundings for your plants (ideas from Duro-Lite).

1. Where natural light is available, but not enough of it, supplement with incandescent spots or fluorescent lights, using them in the afternoon and evening. That way you won't have to leave the lights on for a full 14 to 16 hours, and at the same time you can enjoy the plants fully at night, a time when they would normally be lost in dim shadow.

2. Provide reflective surfaces around as much of your light-grown greenery as possible—even beneath plants. Experiments have shown that soybeans and corn grown under fluorescent lights increase their yield by as much as 30 percent when a reflective mulch such as aluminum foil is used over the soil. So use white quartz chips or another reflective material in your pebble tray and on your pot tops.

3. Change your horticultural fluorescent tubes every 12 months, even if they look all right. After a year's use, especially if they run for 14 to 16 hours a day, their efficiency will be greatly reduced. Cleaning the lamps and reflectors once a month is also a good idea.

4. Make light gardening part of your decorating scheme. Place a light garden in a bath or powder room, stairwell, and other locations where the family traffic is heavy and the on-and-off switches of your house lights are constantly going—or forgotten. In the long run it uses hardly any extra electricity.

5. Everyone deserves a vacation. Shut down part of your light garden in the summer and put the plants outside. The wind and rain will clean both plants and pots. Acclimatize the plants slowly. Do not place them in direct sunlight for the first few days. When bringing the plants back indoors check them for insects. Most pests can be removed by swabbing the leaves with alcohol-soaked cotton balls.

6. You can achieve a pleasant visual effect with Plant Lites by interspersing them with other bulbs.

7. Make sure that if you are using incandescent lights they do not raise the temperature on the plant to higher than 80 degrees F. Seventy-five degrees is about perfect. You can raise or lower the plants on blocks to make sure they are the proper distance from the light bulbs and, therefore, at the best temperature. Incandescents used to light plants in a window help mitigate the effects of the cold during wintertime, allowing plant-decorated windows even in climates with very low temperatures.

Planter Shelf

With lighting and a surrounding of mirror tiles, an ordinary shelf can become a planter that is the perfect display space for your favorites (suggestions by Dow-Corning).

Tools and materials. Dow Corning silicone rubber sealant; mirror tiles to cover back and sides of shelf; Gro-Lite to install at shelf top.

Redwood Hanging Planter Platform

You can alter the dimensions of this airy planter at will, but the size given (14" x 16¾") is ideal for one average hanging plant pot. Make a cluster of platforms that hang at different heights, put all together (from the California Redwood Association).

Tools and materials. Three pieces of redwood 2" x 4" x 14"; three pieces of redwood 1" x 2" x 16¾"; ½ pint glue; four screw eyes; cord or rope. (Actual dimensions of 1x2s may be ¾" x 1⅝".)

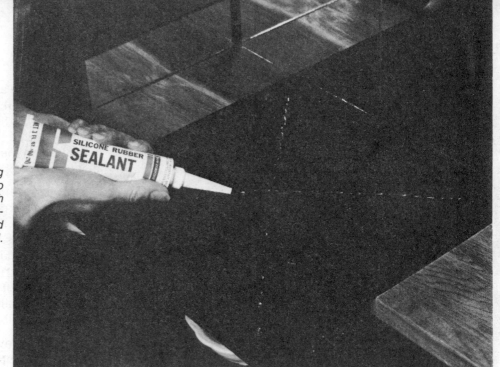

1. *Run beads of sealant criss-crossing the backs of mirror tiles and press into place. This adhesive stands up to both heat and moisture, and fills in any unevenness in the tiles or the background so that the mirror tiles are not stressed.*

2. *To prevent moisture from leaking between shelf joints, run a bead of silicone in all corners of the shelf. Because silicone sealant is flexible, expansion and contraction of joints won't affect the sealant.*

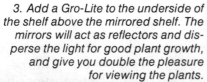

3. *Add a Gro-Lite to the underside of the shelf above the mirrored shelf. The mirrors will act as reflectors and disperse the light for good plant growth, and give you double the pleasure for viewing the plants.*

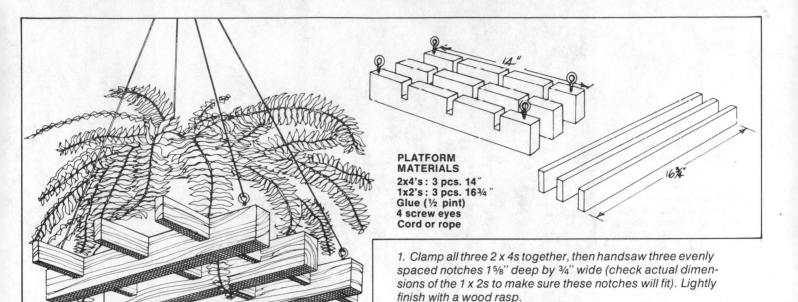

PLATFORM MATERIALS
2x4's : 3 pcs. 14"
1x2's : 3 pcs. 16¾"
Glue (½ pint)
4 screw eyes
Cord or rope

1. Clamp all three 2 x 4s together, then handsaw three evenly spaced notches 1⅝" deep by ¾" wide (check actual dimensions of the 1 x 2s to make sure these notches will fit). Lightly finish with a wood rasp.
2. Apply cross pieces (1 x 2s) with glue only and let set overnight.
3. Install screw eyes for cord or rope on four corners of 2 x 4s.

Two-Pot Redwood Planter Stand

From the top, this planter stand looks like a child's whirlygig. From the front, it is a handsome but casual planter (from the California Redwood Association). The planter is 40" high and 17¾" wide.

Tools and materials. Four pieces of redwood 1" x 4" x 40"; two pieces of redwood 1" x 4" x 17¾"; 12 pieces of redwood 1" x 4" x 8½"; eight pieces of redwood 1" x 2" x 3½"; ½ pint of glue; 6d nails (about 16); ¼" x 2½" bolts and nuts (about eight).

Pointers for Working with Redwood

Exact lumber dimensions can be cut from 1 x 2s, 1 x 4s, 1 x 6s, and 2 x 4s, available in 4' to 10' lengths. Assemble all these projects with resorcinol, formaldehyde glue (waterproof, not "water resistant"), and noncorrosive hot-dipped galvanized, aluminum or stainless steel nails and galvanized screws, bolts, and nuts. Pre-drill all nail holes with a drill bit three-quarters the diameter of the nail you plan to use.

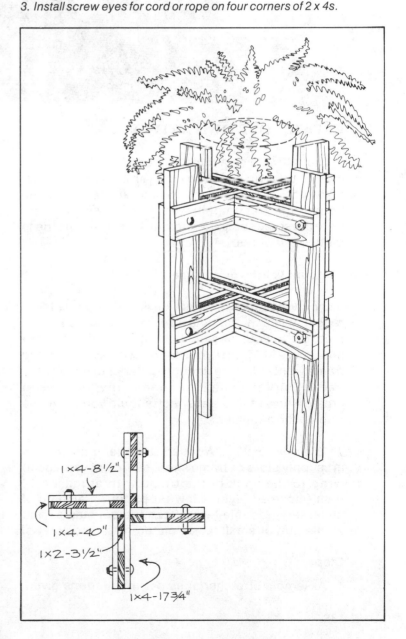

1. To assemble each cross section, start with 1 x 4 that is 17¾" long. Attach to opposite sides one 1 x 4, 8½" long, separated from long 1 x 4 toward the center by a 1 x 2 support cleat 3½" long, gluing and nailing.
2. Butt join one 1 x 4, 8½" long to combined support cleat and 1 x 4 already attached at the center. Add support cleat to new 1 x 4 and another 1 x 4. Each cross section takes six 1 x 4s 8½" long, and four 1 x 2 support cleats 3½" long. Glue and nail all joinings.
3. Attach legs with nuts and bolts centered where cross sections cross legs. Legs go in between cross section "wings." Top of higher cross section is 36" from ground; top of lower cross section is 18" from ground.

You can mount fabrics on frames of the same size for little cost. Note how attractive the modern abstract design looks with the traditional three-candle lamp. (Lamp by Stieffel)

CREATE YOUR OWN ARTWORK

That attractive painting you admired may well be mounted fabric bought by the yard. And the special textured wall hanging may well be an area rug, artistic enough to compete with an exclusive design. Here are some special techniques for mounting these modern artworks.

Mount Fabrics on a Frame

By choosing an abstract design that has a large repeat, you can combine a series of mounted fabric pictures in your personal variation of the modern multiples. Plan how your fabric will lay out on the frame front, allowing enough material to wrap to the back. You then can interchange the pictures to create a new multiple abstract, should you tire of the original arrangement.

Tools and materials. Wooden stretcher bars from an art supply store or frame shop; sufficient yardage to wrap to the back of the frame with at least a 1'' hem (make sure you allow for pattern matching, if necessary); double-faced Scotch tape; staples and staple gun or small tacks; picture wire and screws.

Steps

1. Assemble stretcher(s) as per instructions given.

You can find them premitered and premeasured.

2. Measure and cut material allowing at least enough to wrap around with a 1'' hem on back of stretcher. Make sure that the pattern is centered as you wish on the stretcher/frame before cutting. One method is to place fabric over stretcher, face side up. Mark corners with pins. Slide stretcher out, lay fabric flat, and measure and mark distance from corners and sides on fabric to establish cut lines.

3. Place double-stick tape on front side of stretcher/frame. Press fabric onto double-stick tape to keep it properly positioned on the front.

4. Place fabric and frame face down on a clean surface. Use staples or small tacks to secure at center top, working out on either side to just before corner. Check that fabric is secured straight, and staple along the bottom from center out, making sure fabric is taut. Staple/secure sides from centers toward corners.

5. To finish corners, smooth fabric along the top stretcher bar. Make a neat mitered fold and staple it into place at each corner. Repeat the process for bottom stretcher bar.

6. Bring side corner material over and smooth it into a sharp corner over top and bottom mitered folds. Staple it into place to finish corners.

Designer Michael Love used muted oyster colored all wool carpet to cover oblong tables and shelves running along the back of a pair of sofas. Next, she hung a handsome area rug designed by Milo Baughman on the wall as its own artwork. (Carpeting and area rug from Bigelow-Sanford, Inc.)

Mounting a Rug or other Heavy Textile

The procedure is similar to that for mounting fabric on stretchers, but you may want to attach heavy material only to side of stretchers without wrapping a bulky mass to the back.

Staples are invisible for certain kinds of heavy textiles. For lighter weights, substitute small nails. Hammer them halfway in, then cut off heads with pliers and hammer in until they are out of sight.

Providing a frame for heavy textile hangings gives them a neater appearance. It also prolongs the life of the hanging by helping to distribute the weight instead of having it all suspend from the top edge. If you like the material well enough to hang it in the first place, then hang it in such a way that no damage is done in the process.

139

Pictures with light and dark frames and mats that echo the colors of their neighbors make even this staircase grouping homogeneous. (Design by Richard W. Jones for Eastman Kodak Co.)

PLANNING PICTURE GROUPINGS

Getting it all together is the best way of displaying your oddments of collected photos, prints, or other memorabilia. Using matching frames and starting with a total plan are the two simplest means of taking an assortment of artworks and making one big decorative statement (suggestions from the Western Wood Moulding and Millwork Producers).

—Start by envisioning the outside shape that you want to create with the pictures. A recognizable rectangle, square, oval, circle, or shape that exactly fits the particular wall space is better than an arrangement without clear border definitions.

—Create at least one strong vertical and one strong horizontal element.

—Balance light and dark frames, heavy and slight frames throughout the arrangement.

If you use a shelf along the wall to support pictures at eye level, you can mix photographs and figurines. (Designed by Richard W. Jones for Eastman Kodak Co.)

—Lay out your grouping before attaching anything to the wall. Various methods include marking off space on the floor and arranging actual elements on it; making a layout on graph paper with each artwork cut out of a piece of separate paper and identified, so you can push the pieces around; and making a full-sized mock-up by using brown paper to represent each artwork, which you can then temporarily tape to the wall.

—Consider using other items in your picture groupings to give relief and freshness to the arrangement. Plates or oval-shaped objects add variety, as do mirrors.

—Keep in mind any other elements that will influence the arrangement, such as hanging lamps or plants, or furniture that might appear within the arrangement.

CREATIVE FLOOR TREATMENTS

Custom floor covering treatments are relatively easy with new do-it-yourself materials. Both carpet and resilient flooring tiles are designed for quick application and ease of handling by novices as well as the experienced. Some also are backed with materials and constructed so that they can be applied over many kinds of flooring, including flooring below grade.

Be Inventive with Resilient Tiles

To depart from the ordinary, create your own effects with tiles instead of merely laying matched tiles all in rows. Good instructions covering the mechanics of laying self-stick tiles are available with the tiles when you purchase them. To create a pattern of your own design, however, you will want to start by making a layout on paper. That allows you to see what the overall effect will be and also to make sure you can order the right number of tiles of each design or color. Include in your plans and on the layout the dimensions of any feature strips that you might want to incorporate. These can be purchased pre-cut ½", 1", and 2" widths. Srips are generally 2' long and come in solid colors.

Here are some ideas to get started. Choose one of these suggestions or invent your own design.

—Arrange four tiles in a square, and separate them with strips for a large tattersall plaid effect.

—Use strips to set off one area that needs special emphasis, such as the floor extending 2' in front of a bar or fireplace. You could even use a different color for this smaller area.

—Simulate a contrasting color "rug" for part of the flooring by using a separate color and bordering it with strips.

—Use the simple, classic checkerboard alternation of two different colors of square tiles.

—Create a herringbone effect by placing two matched tiles side by side, alternating them with two contrasting tiles. Alternate the next row color for color, in sets of two's.

—Create a large square of four tiles and alternate this block with ones of a different color for a large checkerboard effect.

—Surround one tile with eight tiles of a different color in a square, then reverse the combination for the next section.

—Use half-tiles cut on the diagonal for an infinite variety of patterns based on patchwork quilt designs.

—Lay all tiles diagonally instead of parallel to the walls.

Manufacturer's List

We are grateful to the following companies for providing us with the material and other related information for this book.

Allied Chemical Corp.
Fibers Division
1441 Broadway
New York, NY 10018

American Olean Tile Co.
Lansdale, PA 19446

American Standard
P.O. Box 2003
New Brunswick, NJ 08903

Armstrong Cork Co.
Lancaster, PA 17604

Azrock Floor Products
P.O. Box 531
San Antonio, TX 78292

Belgian Linen Association
280 Madison Avenue
New York, NY 10016

Bigelow-Sanford, Inc.
P.O. Box 3089
Greenville, SC 29602

California Redwood Association
617 Montgomery St.
San Francisco, CA 94111

Callaway Area Rugs
Milliken
1 Dallis St.
LaGrange, GA 30240

Classic Leather/Vangard
Box 2884
Hickory, NC 28601

Con-Tact Vinyl by
Comark Plastics Division
3601 Hempstead Turnpike
Levittown, NY 11756

Dow Corning Corp.
Midland, MI 48640

Drawermaster
Drawer Kit Sales
Box 36
Alden, MI 49612

Duro-Lite Lamps, Inc.
17-10 Willow St.
Fair Lawn, NJ 07410

Eastman Kodak Co.
343 State Street
Rochester, NY 14650

Environmental Graphics
1117 Vicksburg Land No.
Wayzata, MN 55391

Ethan Allen, Inc.
Ethan Allen Drive
Danbury, CN 06810

Focal Point, Inc.
4820 S. Atlanta Rd.
Smyra, GA 30080

General Electric Lamp
   Business Group
General Electric Company
Nela Park
Cleveland, OH 44112

Georgia-Pacific Corp.
900 S.W. Fifth Avenue
Portland, OR 97204

Goodyear Tire & Rubber Co.
Akron, OH 44316

Halo Lighting
400 Busse Rd.
Elk Grove Village, IL 60007

Hilo Steiner
507 Broad Street
Shrewsbury, NJ 07701

Howard Miller
806 E. Main Street
Zeeland, MI 49464

James David, Inc.
128 Weldon Parkway
Maryland Heights, MD 63043

James Seeman Studios Inc.
Div. of Masonite Corp.
50 Rose Place
Garden City Park, NY 11040

Joanna Western Mills
261 Fifth Avenue
New York, NY 10016

J. Josephson Inc.
20 Horizon Blvd.
So. Hackensack, NJ 07606

Klise Manufacturing Co.
601 Maryland Ave., N.E.
Grand Rapids, MI 49505

Leviton Manufacturing Co., Inc.
59-25 Little Neck Parkway
Little Neck, NY 11362

Levelor Blinds
Levelor-Lorentzen, Inc.
720 Monroe St.
Hoboken, NJ 07030

Louisiana-Pacific Corp.
1300 S.W. Fifth Avenue
Portland, OR 97201

Masonite Corp.
Dover, OH 44622

Montgomery Ward Co.
Montgomery Ward Plaza
Chicago, IL 60671

1001 Decorating Ideas Magazine
149 Fifth Avenue
New York, NY 10010

Pope & Talbot
1700 S.W. 4th Avenue
Portland, OR 97201

Scandecor, Inc.
430 Pike Rd.
Southhampton, PA 18966

"Scotch-Gard"
3M Company
600 3rd Avenue
New York, NY 10016

The Simmons Co.
One Park Avenue
New York, NY 10016

Springs Mills Inc.
18 W. 40th St.
New York, NY 10010

Stanley Drapery Hardware
The Stanley Works
195 Lake Street
New Britain, CN 06050

Stanley Tools
The Stanley Works
195 Lake Street
New Britain, CN 06054

Stauffer Chemical Co.
Plastics Division
Westport, CN 06880

The Stieffel Company
700 No. Kingsberry St.
Chicago, IL 60610

Sugar Hill Furniture
Lisbon, NH 03585

Thayer Coggin, Inc.
South Road
High Point, NC 27262

United States Gypsum Co.
101 S. Wacker Drive
Chicago, IL 60606

Wallcovering Industry Bureau
Ruder & Finn, Inc.
110 E. 59th St.
New York, NY 10022

Wall-Tex Division
Columbus Coated Fabrics Co.
7th & Grant Avenue
Columbus, OH 43216

Western Wood Moulding &
Millwork Producers Inc.
P.O. Box 25278
1730 S.W. Skyline
Portland, OR 97225

Z-Brick Company
Division of VMC
2834 N.W. Market Street
Seattle, WA 98107

Designers whose work is featured in this book: Rhoda Albom; Milo Baughman; Michael Cannarozzi; Thomas Hill Cook; Evan Frances; Louise Gowan; Lois Monroe Hoyt; J. Christopher Jones; Richard W. Jones; Michael Love; Jim de Martin; Alan Scruggs; Gloria Vanderbilt.

Index